The Growth and Influence of Islam

In the Nations of Asia and Central Asia

Kazakhstan

The Growth and Influence of Islam

IN THE NATIONS OF ASIA AND CENTRAL ASIA

Afghanistan

Azerbaijan

Bangladesh

Indonesia

Islam in Asia: Facts and Figures

Islamism and Terrorist Groups in Asia

Kazakhstan

The Kurds

Kyrgyzstan

Malaysia

Muslims in China

Muslims in India

Muslims in Russia

Pakistan

Tajikistan

Turkmenistan

Uzbekistan

The Growth and Influence of Islam
IN THE NATIONS OF ASIA AND CENTRAL ASIA

Kazakhstan

Jim Corrigan

Mason Crest Publishers
Philadelphia

Produced by OTTN Publishing, Stockton, New Jersey

Mason Crest Publishers
370 Reed Road
Broomall, PA 19008
www.masoncrest.com

First printing

1 3 5 7 9 8 6 4 2

Library of Congress Cataloging-in-Publication Data

Corrigan, Jim.
  Kazakhstan / Jim Corrigan.
    p. cm. — (Growth and influence of Islam in the nations of Asia and
Central Asia)
  Includes bibliographical references and index.
  ISBN 1-59084-882-9
  1. Kazakhstan—Juvenile literature. I. Title. II. Series.
  DK903.C67 2005
  958.45—dc22

                                2004022664

Table of Contents

Dr. Harvey Sicherman, president and director of the Foreign Policy Research Institute, is the author of such books as *America the Vulnerable: Our Military Problems and How to Fix Them* (2002) and *Palestinian Autonomy, Self-Government and Peace* (1993).

Introduction

by Dr. Harvey Sicherman

America's triumph in the Cold War promised a new burst of peace and prosperity. Indeed, the decade between the demise of the Soviet Union and the destruction of September 11, 2001, proved deceptively hopeful. Today, of course, we are more fully aware—to our sorrow—of the dangers and troubles no longer just below the surface.

The Muslim identities of most of the terrorists at war with the United States have also provoked great interest in Islam as well as the role of religion in politics. It is crucial for Americans not to assume that Osama bin Laden's ideas are identical to those of most Muslims or, for that matter, that most Muslims are Arabs. A truly world religion, Islam claims hundreds of millions of adherents, from every ethnic group scattered across the globe. This book series covers the growth and influence of Muslims in Asia and Central Asia.

A glance at the map establishes the extraordinary coverage of our authors. Every climate and terrain may be found, along with every form of human society, from the nomadic groups of the Central Asian steppes to highly sophisticated cities such as Singapore, New Delhi, and Shanghai. The economies of the nations examined in this series are likewise highly diverse. In some, barter systems are still used; others incorporate modern stock markets. In some of the countries, large oil reserves hold out the prospect of prosperity. Other countries, such as India and China, have progressed by moving from a government-controlled to a more market-based economic system. Still other countries have built wealth on service and shipping.

Central Asia and Asia is a heavily armed and turbulent area. Three of its states (China, India, and Pakistan) are nuclear powers, and one (Kazakhstan) only recently rid itself of nuclear weapons. But it is also a place where the horse and mule remain indispensable instruments of war. All of the region's states have an extensive history of conflict, domestic and international, old and new. Afghanistan, for example, has known little but invasion and civil war over the past two decades.

Governments include dictatorships, democracies, and hybrids without a name; centralized and decentralized administrations; and older patterns of tribal and clan associations. The region is a veritable encyclopedia of political expression.

Although such variety defies easy generalities, it is still possible to make several observations. First, the geopolitics of Central Asia and Asia reflect the impact of empires and the struggles of post-imperial independence. Central Asia, a historic corridor for traders and soldiers, was the scene of Russian expansion well into Soviet times. While Kazakhstan's leaders participated in the historic meeting of December 25, 1991, that dissolved the Soviet Union, the rest of the region's newly independent republics hardly expected it. They have found it difficult to grapple with a sometimes tenuous independence, buffeted by a strong residual Russian influence, the absence of settled institutions, the temptation of newly valuable natural resources, and mixed populations lacking a solid national identity. The shards of the Soviet Union have often been sharp—witness the Russian war in Chechnya—and sometimes fatal for those ambitious to grasp them.

**A Canadian oil company owns this group of petroleum tanks in Shymkent.
Since becoming independent in 1991, Kazakhstan has invited foreigners to
invest in developing its vast oil reserves.**

Moving further east, one encounters an older devolution, that of the
half-century since the British Raj dissolved into India and Pakistan (the
latter giving violent birth to Bangladesh in 1971). Only recently, partly
under the impact of the war on terrorism, have these nuclear-armed neighbors and adversaries found it possible to renew attempts at reconciliation.
Still further east, Malaysia shares a British experience, but Indonesia has
been influenced by its Dutch heritage. Even China defines its own borders
along the lines of the Qing empire (the last pre-republican dynasty) at its

most expansionist (including Tibet and Taiwan). These imperial histories lie heavily upon the politics of the region.

A second aspect worth noting is the variety of economic experimentation afoot in the area. State-dominated economic strategies, still in the ascendant, are separating government from the actual running of commerce and industry. "Privatization," however, is frequently a byword for crony capitalism and corruption. Yet in dynamic economies such as that of China, as well as an increasingly productive India, hundreds of millions of people have dramatically improved both their standard of living and their hope for the future. All of them aspire to benefit from international trade. Competitive advantages, such as low-cost labor (in some cases trained in high technology) and valuable natural resources (oil, gas, and minerals), promise much. This is indeed a revolution of rising expectations, some of which are being satisfied.

Yet more than corruption threatens this progress. Population increase, even though moderating, still overwhelms educational and employment opportunities. Many countries are marked by extremes of wealth and poverty, especially between rural and urban areas. Dangerous jealousies threaten ethnic groups (such as anti-Chinese violence in Indonesia). Hopelessly overburdened public services portend turmoil. Public health, never adequate, is harmed further by environmental damage to critical resources (such as the Aral Sea). By and large, Central Asian and Asian countries are living well beyond their infrastructures.

Third and finally, Islam has deeply affected the states and peoples of the region. Indonesia is the largest Muslim state in the world, and India hosts the second-largest Muslim population. Islam is not only the official religion of many states, it is the very reason for Pakistan's existence. But Islamic practices and groups vary: the well-known Sunni and Shiite groups are joined by energetic Salafi (Wahabi) and Sufi movements. Over the last 20 years especially, South and Central Asia have become battlegrounds for competing Shiite (Iranian) and Wahabi (Saudi) doctrines, well financed from abroad and aggressively antagonistic toward non-Muslims and each other. Resistance to the Soviet invasion of Afghanistan brought these groups battle-tested warriors and organizers. The war on terrorism has exposed just how far-reaching and active the new advocates of holy war (jihad) can be. Indonesia, in particular, is the scene of rivalry between an older, tolerant Islam and the jihadists. But Pakistan also faces an Islamic identity crisis. And India, wracked by sectarian strife, must hold together its democratic framework despite Muslim and Hindu extremists. This newly significant struggle within Islam, superimposed on an older Muslim history, will shape political and economic destinies throughout the region and beyond. Hence, the focus of our series.

We hope that these books will enlighten both teacher and student about a critical subject in a critical area of the world. Central Asia and Asia would be important in their own right to Americans; arguably, after 9/11, they became vital to our national security. And the enduring impact of Islam is a crucial factor we must understand. We at the Foreign Policy Research Institute hope these books will illuminate both the facts and the prospects.

Kazakhstan's President Nursultan Nazarbayev (center) leaves a polling station in Astana after casting his ballot in the country's September 2004 parliamentary election. Although Kazakhstan has some of the trappings of democracy, such as competing political parties and national elections, independent observers claim that Nazarbayev and his cronies have so much control that elections are a sham.

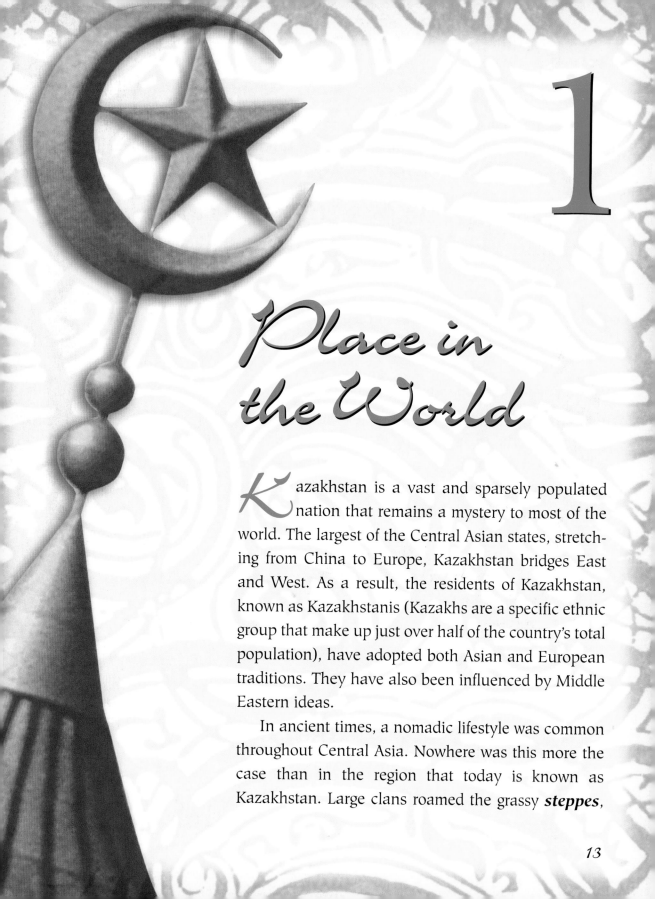

1

Place in the World

*K*azakhstan is a vast and sparsely populated nation that remains a mystery to most of the world. The largest of the Central Asian states, stretching from China to Europe, Kazakhstan bridges East and West. As a result, the residents of Kazakhstan, known as Kazakhstanis (Kazakhs are a specific ethnic group that make up just over half of the country's total population), have adopted both Asian and European traditions. They have also been influenced by Middle Eastern ideas.

In ancient times, a nomadic lifestyle was common throughout Central Asia. Nowhere was this more the case than in the region that today is known as Kazakhstan. Large clans roamed the grassy *steppes*, which served as ideal grazing lands for their livestock. A migratory, pastoral way of life characterized the people for centuries. They practiced it until the 1920s, when political events forced them to settle.

Islam was relatively slow to arrive in the Kazakhstan region. The religion had existed for hundreds of years before finally penetrating the nomadic population around the 12th century. (By contrast, some people in other parts of Central Asia converted to Islam as early as the 8th century.) The nomads gradually accepted Islam, but viewed it more as a set of principles than a formal religion. As a traveling people, they had little incentive to build stone **mosques**, though clans often carried a copy of the **Qur'an**, the holy book of Islam, on their journeys. Today, roughly half of Kazakhstan's population practices Islam, but these people observe the religion's tenets in a less-rigid manner than do Muslims in other parts of the world. In fact, a 1997 study by the U.S. Information Agency found that less than half of Kazakhstani Muslims could list the basic principles and beliefs of Islam. Despite this Muslims in Kazakhstan still identify closely with Muslims of other countries.

The country's residents are a diverse people. In addition to the ethnic Kazakhs who are descended from the nomadic clans, Kazakhstan today is home to ethnic Russians, Ukrainians, Uzbeks, Germans, Koreans, and other groups. This diversity of population is a direct result of the policies that Russian imperialists and Soviet officials implemented during the 18th, 19th, and 20th centuries.

Strong Ties to Russia

Kazakhstan was the first Central Asian region to be absorbed into the sprawling Russian empire, which in 1922 became the Union of Soviet Socialist Republics (U.S.S.R.). During nearly 70 years of Soviet rule, a variety of peoples migrated into Kazakhstan. Some people came voluntarily, while others were forcibly relocated there by the Soviet government.

Although today tension exists between native and foreign groups, ethnic violence in Kazakhstan is rare.

The Soviet Union was founded on the principles of **communism**, a political theory in which there are no social classes and no private property; instead, all members of the community share ownership of all property and wealth. In the Soviet Union, the government, which claimed to represent the people, took over all of the businesses and factories and rigidly controlled all aspects of life within the state. Soviet citizens were told to work together for the common good, and promised an equal share in the fruits of their labor. However, the independent-minded Kazakhstanis disliked the Soviet approach and strongly resisted communist ideology. In the 1920s, when Soviet officials tried to seize livestock for

Nazarbayev (second from left) speaks with (left to right) President Alexander Lukashenko of Belarus, President Vladimir Putin of Russia, and President Leonid Kuchma of Ukraine at a 2004 conference in Astana. Since independence, Kazakhstan has maintained close ties with Russia, as well as with other former Soviet republics.

government-owned farms, most clans responded by slaughtering their own herds. The resistance was ultimately unsuccessful, and the Kazakhs were forced to give up their nomadic lifestyle and settle on government farms.

The Soviets also tried to stamp out the practice of Islam and other religions, considering it a threat to government authority. Despite the government restrictions, many Kazakhstani Muslims refused to abandon their religion and secretly continued to practice it.

Soviet rule was hard on the people of Kazakhstan. In addition to controlling its citizens' lives, the government often displayed an appalling lack of concern for their welfare. For example, during the 1950s northeastern Kazakhstan became the primary testing ground for Soviet nuclear weapons. Although thinly populated areas were chosen for the tests, countless Kazakhstanis were exposed to radioactive fallout. Nuclear testing continued into the 1980s, and as a result many people today still suffer from poor health related to radiation exposure.

At the same time, Kazakhstan benefited from inclusion in the U.S.S.R. Schools, hospitals, and housing complexes were built during the Soviet era. Irrigation systems were installed to make farming more productive. A space center constructed in central Kazakhstan became the heart of the Soviet space exploration program. Although Kazakhstanis still resented the government's rigid policies, they enjoyed the modern technology it fostered.

In 1991 the Soviet Union collapsed and Kazakhstan became an independent state. While a new era of independence was a cause for celebration, the people of Kazakhstan were also apprehensive. For more than a century they had lived under Russian domination, and it was difficult to imagine anything else. The Russians had educated and protected them. As a new country, Kazakhstan had no military and an underdeveloped economy.

A popular Kazakh politician named Nursultan Nazarbayev, the former Communist Party leader of the republic, stepped forward to lead the new government as Kazakhstan's first elected president. During his first years in office, the government made several key moves—it worked to establish democratic institutions and ***privatize*** the economy. It also befriended Western nations that could provide financial support. The United States, in particular, was eager to assist Kazakhstan because it was the only Central Asian republic to inherit nuclear weapons from the U.S.S.R. By providing aid, the United States hoped to prevent Kazakhstanis from selling nuclear weapons or weapons-grade material to terrorist organizations or so-called rogue states like Iraq, Iran, North Korea, Libya, and Syria.

Perhaps the government's most important move was maintaining friendly relations with Russia. Nazarbayev acknowledged that although the Soviet Union was gone, Moscow's influence in Central Asia was not. During the Soviet era, the industrial and agricultural production of each republic had been closely controlled by the central government in Moscow. Severing those financial and economic ties would take time. Further, Nazarbayev knew that the Russian military, though weaker than it once was, was still the most powerful force in the region.

Religious Revival, Economic Problems, and Government Corruption

Islam saw a revival in Kazakhstan after independence. Muslims rejoiced in the new freedom to practice their religion openly, and hundreds of mosques were built. The resurgence worried government officials, who feared that religious zealots could possibly stir tension between Muslims and the country's large Christian population, many of whom were ethnic Russians. Such conflict might lead to civil war, and perhaps even an invasion by Moscow to protect the ethnic Russians living in Kazakhstan. Nazarbayev went to great lengths to ensure that his government was ***secular*** and would not be influenced by any religion.

The religious clashes that Kazakhstan's leaders so nervously anticipated never materialized. The public's focus instead shifted to the country's

Traditional Muslim graves line a road near the village of Stariy Karatily. Nearly half of Kazakhstanis follow Islam, the dominant religion of Central Asia.

rapidly deteriorating economy, which impacted Kazakhstanis of all faiths and backgrounds. Kazakhstan has a wealth of natural resources, which provide a tremendous opportunity for prosperity and economic growth. The country has always been known to contain large untapped reserves of natural gas and petroleum, as well as major deposits of minerals and precious metals. Exploration during the mid-1990s revealed that these reserves are even greater than first believed. Western oil companies, which had long expressed interest in tapping Kazakhstan's petroleum, began courting government officials for drilling rights.

Initially, however, the shock of privatization and other sweeping economic changes in the republic was more than Kazakhstan's fragile economy could handle. Prices rose and unemployment soared while the average household income dropped. A typical family could barely afford a sufficient amount of food, much less other goods and services.

In recent years, economic conditions have gradually improved as revenue from oil flows into the country. However, the benefits of increased oil production and other economic changes have been felt by relatively few people, and overall Kazakhstan's development has been stunted by greed. The government of Kazakhstan is notoriously corrupt. Friends and family members of political leaders benefited the most from the privatization of businesses and industries. Bribery is commonplace, and dishonest officials routinely divert public money into their own private accounts. President Nazarbayev is believed to be one of the worst offenders. Before entering politics, he was a common laborer in a metallurgy plant. Now he is thought to be among the richest men in the world.

Early in his presidency, Nazarbayev recognized that a multiparty democracy was far more difficult to control than the Soviet Union's single-party political system. He gradually backed away from his initial promises to cultivate democracy, concentrating instead on consolidating his own power. In 1995, after Kazakhstan's parliament refused to obey his wishes, he dissolved it and created a new legislature more to his liking. He also modified the nation's constitution to give the president more power, and began installing close friends and family members in positions of authority.

Today, Kazakhstan's government stands somewhere between democracy and dictatorship. Common citizens have seen little financial improvement in their lives since independence, and some actually look back fondly on Soviet rule. Meanwhile, an elite few have grown extremely wealthy through practices involving corruption and favoritism. Similar conditions in other countries have led to such problems as social unrest, religious extremism, and terrorism. It is uncertain whether the country will face the same problems, or whether a new course will unfold in Kazakhstan.

The sun rises over a quiet lake near Shagen, Kazakhstan. The country has an extensive system of lakes and rivers.

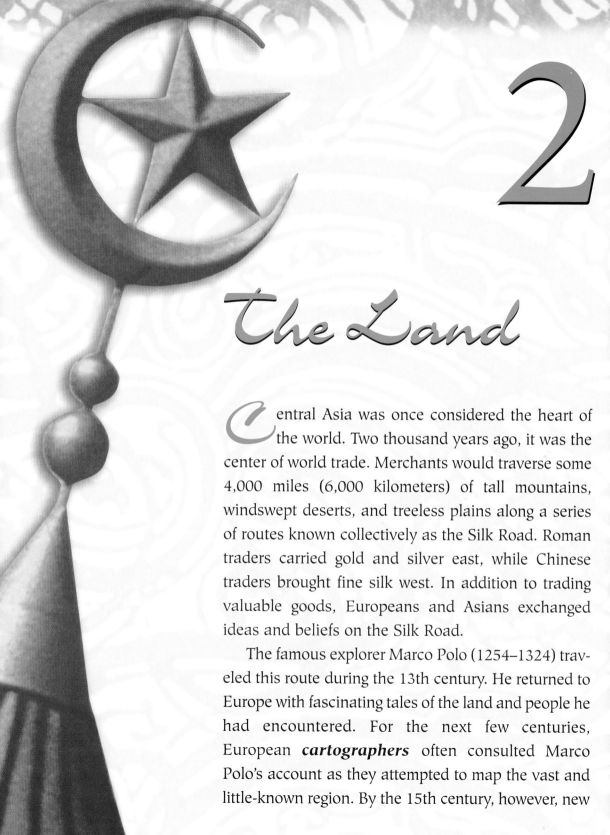

2

The Land

Central Asia was once considered the heart of the world. Two thousand years ago, it was the center of world trade. Merchants would traverse some 4,000 miles (6,000 kilometers) of tall mountains, windswept deserts, and treeless plains along a series of routes known collectively as the Silk Road. Roman traders carried gold and silver east, while Chinese traders brought fine silk west. In addition to trading valuable goods, Europeans and Asians exchanged ideas and beliefs on the Silk Road.

The famous explorer Marco Polo (1254–1324) traveled this route during the 13th century. He returned to Europe with fascinating tales of the land and people he had encountered. For the next few centuries, European *cartographers* often consulted Marco Polo's account as they attempted to map the vast and little-known region. By the 15th century, however, new seaborne trade routes made the Silk Road obsolete. Central Asia became a forgotten and dangerous land visited only by rugged adventurers.

This region is a place of extremes. Although largely arid, Central Asia is home to the Caspian Sea, the largest inland body of water in the world. The climate varies from exceedingly hot and dry to bitterly cold. Flat, featureless terrain is interrupted by the occasional oasis and enormous mountain ranges.

Kazakhstan occupies the northern two-thirds of Central Asia. Next to Russia, it is the largest of the former Soviet republics. With a total area over a million square miles (more than 2.7 million square kilometers), it is the ninth-largest nation in the world. The country is roughly the size of Western Europe, or about four times larger than the state of Texas.

In the north, Kazakhstan shares a 4,254-mile (6,846-kilometer) border with Russia. This jagged, meandering boundary is one of the longest international borders in the world. To the east is China, and to the south are the Central Asian nations of Kyrgyzstan, Uzbekistan, and Turkmenistan. In the west Kazakhstan has a lengthy shoreline along the Caspian Sea. However, because the Caspian is an inland body of water, Kazakhstan is a landlocked nation with no direct access to ocean routes.

Kazakhstan contains a handful of major cities and a number of smaller ones. Astana, located in the north-central region, is the nation's capital. Almaty, in the southeast, is the country's largest city and a major business center. Most other Kazakh cities sprang up around a major industry, such as coal mining, metallurgy, or petroleum production. Outside these population centers, the country is very sparsely inhabited. Kazakhstan's population density is less than 10 people per square mile (or 4 people per square kilometer).

Geographical Features

The western areas surrounding the Caspian Sea are extremely low and flat. The Karagiye Depression (or Vpadina Kaundy) in the southwest is

Herdsmen watch over their sheep on the grasslands of Kazakhstan.

Kazakhstan's lowest point at 433 feet (132 meters) below sea level.

The country's northern region consists of immense, grassy plains, which are similar to those of the American Midwest. Hearty, deep-rooted plants such as wormwood and tamarisk (also known as salt cedar) help prevent soil erosion on the windswept steppes. The steppes' native grasses were once crucial to the livestock-based cultures of Kazakhstan's past. Today, the raising of grain crops takes priority, and the steppes are the country's breadbasket. Numerous cotton fields also dot the landscape.

Grazing animals and small predators thrive in the plains environment. Foxes and badgers roam the steppes in search of rodents and other prey, while packs of wolves hunt deer and antelope. The saiga antelope is extremely rare and the Kazakh government has taken steps to protect it.

The steppe climate is usually cold, with winter temperatures that can fall below –50° Fahrenheit (–45° Celsius). January temperatures typically

This view of a snow-covered road lined with fir trees was taken in the Ile Alatao National Park near Almaty. The Tian Shan mountains rise in the background.

range from –2°F to 25°F (–19°C to –4°C). A layer of snow typically covers the ground for about 150 days of the year. During the brief summer, thunderstorms dump an average of 10 to 14 inches (25 to 35 centimeters) of rain on the steppes, often producing flash floods. In the warmest month, July, daytime temperatures hover around 70°F (21°C).

The fertile steppes give way to rocky semi-desert before turning into the barren deserts of the south. A variety of small animals, including gophers, sand rats, lizards, and snakes, can be found hiding among the scrub brush. Gazelles are also quite common in the deserts. Temperatures climb as high as 113°F (45°C) while annual rainfall only amounts to about 4 inches (10 cm).

Magnificent mountain ranges ring Kazakhstan's eastern and south-eastern borders. The Altay Mountains in the east, which exceed 15,000 feet (4,600 meters), mark the conclusion of the Russian border and the start of the Chinese border. Mountainous terrain continues south along the entire boundary with China. These hills are broken only by the occasional gap or pass. In the southeast lies the Tian Shan mountain range, and it is here that Kazakhstan's borders with China and Kyrgyzstan meet. The Tian Shan also contains Kazakhstan's highest elevation. At 22,950 feet (6,995 meters), Mount Khan-Tengri (or Khan Tangiri Shyngy) is higher than any peak in North America or Europe.

Forests of spruce, cedar, and larch grow thick on Kazakhstan's mountain slopes. The forests are home to brown bears, mountain goats, and the endangered snow leopard, as well as eagles, falcons, and other predatory birds. Most mountain peaks are continuously snowcapped, while the slopes are typically cool with a yearly precipitation of about 60 inches (152 cm). The alpine environment accounts for only 4 percent of the nation's landscape.

Despite the small amounts of rainfall in most areas, Kazakhstan has an extensive system of lakes and rivers. The Ural River bisects the country's northwestern tip as it travels to the Caspian Sea. In the east, the Ili River flows from China into Lake Balkhash, which is the fourth-largest lake in Asia. A dam constructed in 1970 slowed the flow of the Ili River considerably. As a result, Lake Balkhash has grown smaller and shallower.

Similar circumstances have had a disastrous effect on the Aral Sea, which straddles the border between Kazakhstan and Uzbekistan. In the 1960s, Soviet engineers began diverting water from the Syr Dar'ya and Amu Dar'ya (*dar'ya* means "river") for irrigation purposes. The reduced water supply crippled the region surrounding the Aral Sea, which at the time was the world's fourth-largest lake. In less than three decades the Aral shrunk to one-half of its original size. In 1987, it divided into two bodies of water: the Small Aral Sea in the north and the Large Aral Sea in the south. Scientists predict that the Aral will continue to divide into smaller lakes as it slowly dries up.

Natural Resources

Kazakhstan's extensive supply of underground natural resources is spread across the country. Oil and natural gas are found primarily in the west, while coal and precious metal deposits exist mainly in the east. In addition to gold, Kazakhstan possesses large quantities of other highly valued metals such as nickel, cobalt, lead, zinc, and uranium.

Estimates of the size and scope of the country's petroleum reserves vary widely. Geologists concur that Kazakhstan contains massive oil deposits, but they have trouble agreeing on a figure. Crude oil is measured in barrels, and a standard barrel contains 42 gallons (159 liters). Kazakhstan has been proven to possess 26 billion barrels of oil, or about 2.5 percent of the world's proven oil reserves. Estimates of unproven oil reserves in Kazakhstan range from 30 to 60 billion barrels.

The country's proven reserves of natural gas stand at 65 trillion cubic feet (1.8 trillion cubic meters), which is about 1.2 percent of the world's total. Much more natural gas is believed to exist, but geologists are unable to quantify it. Part of the difficulty in estimating Kazakhstan's oil and natural gas reserves stems from the fact that much of these resources lie beneath the Caspian Sea.

Extracting the republic's underground wealth has taken a heavy toll on the environment. For decades, metal smelters and processing mills have emitted harmful pollutants into the air. **Antiquated** oil refineries have contaminated groundwater supplies. The Caspian Sea faces long-term damage from drilling operations. Unfortunately, the injury done by industry is just one item in a long list of environmental problems plaguing Kazakhstan.

Environmental Issues

The lingering effects of Soviet nuclear weapons testing are a major concern. Most tests were conducted near the eastern city of Semey (formerly

The Geography of Kazakhstan

Location: Central Asia, northwest of China; a small portion
    west of the Ural River in easternmost Europe
Area: (slightly less than four times the size of Texas)
    total: 1,049,155 square miles (2,717,300 sq km)
    land: 1,030,815 square miles (2,669,800 sq km)
    water: 18,340 square miles (47,500 sq km)
Borders: China, 953 miles (1,533 km); Kyrgyzstan, 653
    miles (1,051 km); Russia, 4,254 miles (6,846 km);
    Turkmenistan, 236 miles (379 km); Uzbekistan, 1,369
    miles (2,203 km)
Climate: continental, cold winters and hot summers, arid
    and semiarid
Terrain: extends from the Volga to the Altay Mountains
    and from the plains in western Siberia to oases and
    desert in Central Asia
Elevation extremes:
    lowest point: Karagiye Depression (Vpadina Kaundy),
        –433 feet (–132 meters)
    highest point: Mount Khan-Tengri (or Khan Tangiri
        Shynygy), 22,950 feet (6,995 meters)
Natural hazards: earthquakes in the south, mudslides
    around Almaty

Source: Adapted from CIA World Factbook, 2004.

Semipalatinsk). From the 1950s through the 1980s, a total of 468 nuclear tests were carried out in this area, including at least 26 above-ground detonations. Forty more tests were conducted in Kazakhstan's southwestern deserts.

During the earliest days of nuclear testing in the 1950s, little was known about the impact of radioactive fallout. Soviet officials did not evacuate nearby communities, or even warn residents about upcoming tests. Soon these people began showing symptoms of high-level radioactive exposure. Health problems included cancer, digestive and respiratory illnesses, and a variety of mental disorders. Incidences of stillbirth and birth defects also increased dramatically.

For 40 years, the population of the Semey area suffered in silence. By 1989, as the Soviet Union's grip was loosening, Kazakhstanis decided they had suffered long enough. Olzhas Suleimenov, a well-known poet and politician, founded the Nevada-Semey Movement to ban nuclear testing. The group collected more than a million signatures and organized public demonstrations. International organizations added their support, and within months the testing range was closed.

Although the Semey nuclear testing range has been inactive since October 1989, the region remains a radioactive disaster area. Farmland and drinking water are contaminated. High winds stir up radioactive dust clouds. Birth rates have declined, while the rates of birth defects, anemia, and leukemia have increased. One study of the Semey area found that a third of all children and roughly half of the general population suffer from illnesses linked to radioactivity.

In 1997, the United Nations called on the international community to assist Kazakhstan in cleaning up the region. However, such operations have proven extremely difficult. Soviet scientists left behind little documentation of their activities at the testing range, and levels of radioactivity fluctuate across the countryside. Kazakhstan's government estimates that in order to accurately measure the contamination, a total of 54,000 individual soil samples will need to be taken and analyzed.

The Aral Sea crisis has proven just as difficult to address. Half a century ago, the Aral Sea supported 173 bird species. Today, as this saltwater lake slowly vanishes, fewer than 40 bird species survive, and all of the indigenous species are gone. The last of the lake's 24 indigenous fish

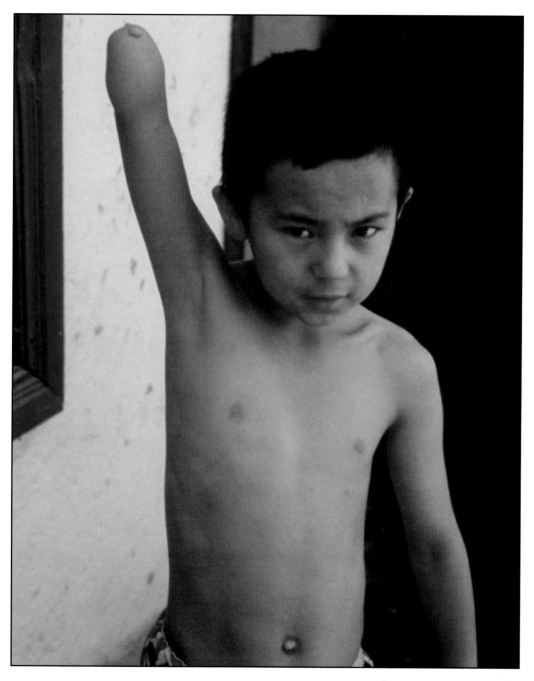

Decades of Soviet-era nuclear tests in eastern Kazakhstan left a horrible legacy: increased rates of birth defects and other health issues caused by radioactive fallout.

species disappeared in the early 1980s. Plant life in the area has also markedly declined.

The Aral's disappearance has had just as serious an impact on the human population. As the sea's shores gradually receded from view, entire fishing communities were abandoned. The rusted hulks of transport ships and fishing boats now sit helplessly in dry sand that is miles from any water.

A man walks across desert land that once was the bed of the Aral Sea. Behind him is a rusted fishing barge left high and dry when the water receded; the coast is now 30 miles (48 km) away from this spot.

Land that was once part of the Aral's lakebed contains a high concentration of salt, making it useless for farming or pastureland. The barren soil also contains chemical fertilizers and pesticides that long ago leaked into the lakebed from the countryside. As this newly created desert dries out, fierce windstorms carry a poisonous mixture of chemicals into the air and deposit it throughout southwestern Kazakhstan.

In 1960, the Aral Sea occupied 25,660 square miles (66,458 sq km) and had an average depth of 53 feet (16 meters). It was about a third as salty as the ocean. The rivers feeding the Aral flowed deep and strong. Farmers along the riverbanks took some of the water to irrigate their farms, but not enough to damage the ecosystem.

A few years later, the government in Moscow decided that Kazakhstan and Uzbekistan needed to significantly boost their cotton production. To achieve this goal, Soviet engineers built massive canals that carried huge volumes of water away from the Syr and Amu rivers. The flow of water reaching the Aral dropped by 90 percent, and the mighty lake began shrinking.

The Aral's depleted condition was largely ignored until the late 1980s, when the lake divided in two. The Central Asian states pledged to cut back on irrigation, thus allowing more water to reach the Aral. The United States, Europe, and the World Bank provided financial support. However, the damage could not be reversed. By 1997 the Aral Sea was barely half its original size and about as salty as the ocean.

Today, financial aid raised in response to the Aral crisis is used primarily to help the victims. People living in the region are constantly exposed to toxic dust, and have higher than normal rates of throat cancer and respiratory illness. Contaminated drinking water is responsible for frequent outbreaks of typhoid and dysentery. The mortality rate in this area is higher than anywhere else in the former Soviet Union.

Preservation of the Large Aral Sea has virtually been abandoned. The volume of water needed to restore it to previous levels is now considered unattainable. The Small Aral Sea, however, stands a better chance for recovery and perhaps even some regrowth, so Kazakhstan's government is focusing its efforts toward that goal.

The Caspian Sea, along Kazakhstan's western border, is currently undergoing a change that is completely different—it is rising at a rate of 6 to 8 inches (14 to 20 cm) each year. The enormous inland sea covers about 143,000 square miles (371,000 sq km), making it roughly 15 times the original size of the Aral Sea. Scientists attribute the Caspian's growth to natural factors, such as increased rainfall, rather than human intervention, but this explanation gives little comfort to the coastal communities that are routinely flooded by the sea's encroaching shoreline.

Pollution is an urgent problem for the Caspian Sea. Intense offshore drilling activity will continue as Kazakhstan and its neighbors exploit the deposits of oil and natural gas beneath the waves. Increased shipping traffic is an additional source of pollution. As the lake slowly rises, its waters may spread into abandoned oil fields and other harmful areas. Pollution poses a serious threat to the Caspian's ecosystem, and therefore to the fishing industry that depends upon it. The sea is the world's chief source of caviar, a delicacy made of fish eggs, for example.

Kazakhstan's waterways continue to suffer from decades of aggressive farming techniques on land. In addition to heavy irrigation, the Soviet cotton plan called for excessive use of fertilizers and pesticides. The natural grasses of the steppes were cleared away, leading to soil erosion. Wind and rain deposited the chemical-laden topsoil into the fragile ecosystems of streams, lakes, marshes, and rivers. Meanwhile, as the depleted earth became less fertile, farmers responded either by adding more fertilizers to the soil, or by clearing new tracts of grassland for farming. The result was a continuing cycle of soil erosion and water pollution.

Kazakhstan's aging industries are chiefly responsible for the worsening air pollution problem. Harmful emissions from outdated metal-processing facilities and energy plants hang over cities as thick smog. Locally based and international environmental groups have pressured the government to implement emission controls. However, officials in Astana are hesitant to take any measures that might slow the nation's economic recovery. Government reluctance, combined with a severe shortage of funding, will likely cause Kazakhstan's environmental troubles to last well into the future.

A Soviet Soyuz spacecraft and launch vehicle wait on the launch pad at the Baykonur complex in Kazakhstan. During the 1960s and 1970s, Baykonur was the world's largest space center.

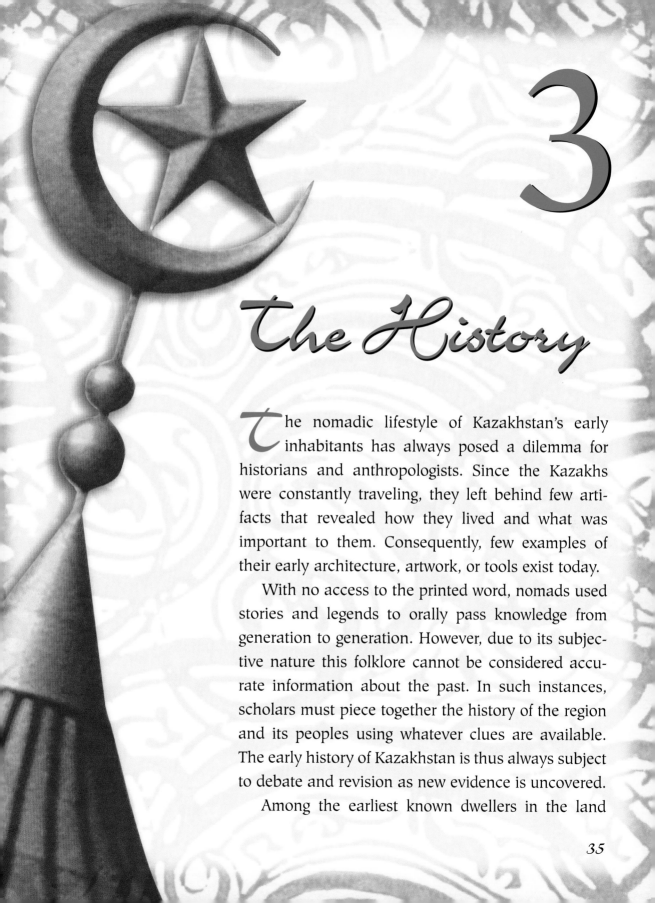

3

The History

The nomadic lifestyle of Kazakhstan's early inhabitants has always posed a dilemma for historians and anthropologists. Since the Kazakhs were constantly traveling, they left behind few artifacts that revealed how they lived and what was important to them. Consequently, few examples of their early architecture, artwork, or tools exist today.

With no access to the printed word, nomads used stories and legends to orally pass knowledge from generation to generation. However, due to its subjective nature this folklore cannot be considered accurate information about the past. In such instances, scholars must piece together the history of the region and its peoples using whatever clues are available. The early history of Kazakhstan is thus always subject to debate and revision as new evidence is uncovered.

Among the earliest known dwellers in the land

now called Kazakhstan was a people known as the Scythians. The Scythians are believed to have spread across much of Central Asia as early as the eighth century B.C. They raised cattle and sheep, traveled in horse-drawn wagons, and crafted fine metalwork. The Scythians repelled a Greek invasion in the fourth century B.C., and took part in many other battles. By the first century B.C., most Scythians had left Central Asia for northern India.

For over a thousand years afterward, tribes and clans of varying origin roamed the Kazakhstan region, but no one group dominated the region. Emperors of Persia and China occasionally sent forces into Central Asia during this time, hoping to gain control of the precious Silk Road trading route. However, no empire established a lasting presence over the territory of present-day Kazakhstan.

In A.D. 751, Chinese and Arab armies clashed in the Talas Valley near Kazakhstan's modern-day border with Kyrgyzstan. The Muslim Arabs were victorious, and their triumph opened the way for Islam—a religion that had emerged from the desert of the Arabian Peninsula less than 150 years earlier—to spread into Central Asia. However, most of those who converted to Islam lived in the southern part of the region. It would be centuries before Islam would establish a presence on the steppes of Kazakhstan.

In 1219, the Mongol conqueror Genghis Khan swept through Central Asia. With an army of 200,000 battle-hardened men, he easily destroyed the scant resistance he encountered. The defeated clans were given a choice between death and loyalty to Genghis Khan; as a result the people of Central Asia became part of his broad empire. Although Mongol rule was harsh, it served to unify the many nomadic clans of the grasslands into a larger political entity for the first time.

When Genghis Khan died in 1227, his empire was divided among his heirs into four smaller kingdoms, called khanates. Genghis's grandson,

Batu Khan, took control over the portion containing present-day Kazakhstan, which became known as the khanate of the Golden Horde. The Golden Horde gradually gained control over most of Russia and eastern Europe. In the early 14th century, the leaders of the khanate became Muslims, and they made Islam the official religion of their kingdom.

The Golden Horde fell into a period of decline after the middle of the 14th century. Tokhtamish Khan, who ruled from 1383 to 1391, reunited the khanate and sacked Moscow, but his rule was threatened by the emergence of another strong leader, Timur Lenk (known in the West as Tamerlane). Timur was a Tatar, a member of a Turkic ethnic group of Central Asia that had participated in the Mongol conquests; in fact, he

Timur Lenk (1336–1405) was a ruthless and brutal military leader. By the time of his death he had conquered a vast Central Asian empire that included present-day Kazakhstan.

claimed to be descended from Genghis Khan. His soldiers waged a series of wars against the Golden Horde in the late 14th century, from which the khanate never recovered. By the middle of the next century, the Golden Horde had fragmented into a number of smaller khanates.

Through the intermarriage of Tatars and Mongols during the 14th and 15th centuries, the Kazakhs emerged as a distinct group with their own lifestyle. Other ethnic groups that had been ruled by the Golden Horde, such as the Uzbeks, settled as farmers, but the Kazakhs chose to remain nomadic.

By the early 16th century, the Kazakh people established their own united khanate. Initially, the Kazakh Khanate flourished. Under the leadership of skilled rulers such as Kasim Khan and Haq Nazar, the many Kazakh clans stayed united. Rich steppe grasses provided the perfect fuel for a horse-mounted army, and Kazakh influence spread throughout the region.

However, there were too many differences among the Kazakh clans and tribes to maintain unity. Following the death of Haq Nazar in 1580, rival factions feuded over who would be the next khan. The disagreements turned bitter and eventually three distinct khanates emerged from the Kazakh Khanate: the Great Horde, the Middle Horde, and the Little Horde. The Great Horde occupied the southeastern region of modern-day Kazakhstan, while the Middle Horde occupied the central steppes and the Little Horde occupied the west. Each horde acted independently and scorned the other two. Individuals were intensely devoted to their horde.

> **Kazakhstan's most prized artifact is a Scythian coat of armor known as "Golden Man." It consists of over 4,000 gold pieces and was discovered in a tomb near Almaty.**

Even today, most ethnic Kazakhs know which horde their ancestors belonged to and take great pride in their lineage.

Russian Intervention

Mongolian tribes to the east soon realized that the divided Kazakhs were no longer as powerful as they had once been. Between 1680 and 1720, a series of Mongolian invasions ravaged the Kazakh hordes. Among the Kazakhs, this period is commonly referred to as the Great Disaster. The weakness of the Kazakhs also encouraged the Chinese Manchu rulers to seize a large part of eastern Kazakh territory in 1771. Desperately, the depleted hordes began looking for help to survive.

To the north, Russia had emerged from centuries of turmoil to become a European power of growing importance under Czar Peter the Great (1672–1725), who opened Russia to the West and established the empire. At first, Russia had little interest in Central Asia, viewing it as an insignificant frontier. The czars were more interested in expanding their empire into eastern Europe and the territories of the Ottoman Empire. Only after each of the Kazakh hordes pledged allegiance to the czar during the 18th century—beginning with the Little Horde in 1731—did Russia grant them protection. In return, the hordes were required to make payments to the czar and defend Russian interests in the area.

The Kazakhs believed they had entered into a mutual defense agreement, but Russia viewed the relationship differently. The Russian czar considered the Kazakh lands to be part of his empire. Russian army forts and settlers steadily appeared in the countryside. Russia's conquest of the Kazakhstan region was gradual, with the territories of the Little Horde and Middle Horde taken initially, and the lands of the Great Horde much later. The Kazakhs periodically rebelled against Russian rule, but each uprising was put down violently. In 1848, Czar Nicholas I introduced a new administrative grid that rendered the division according to hordes obsolete, and

Czar Nicholas I (1796–1855) came to power in 1825. During his reign Kazakhs and other minority groups within the Russian empire were pressured to give up their lifestyles and adopt a Russian way of life. This program, an effort to unite the diverse peoples of the empire, became known as "Russification."

Russia's conquest of Kazakhstan was complete. Throughout the 19th century, the Russian armies conquered the rest of Central Asia.

Russian settlers continued to arrive on the steppes in large numbers. By 1906, more than 140,000 people were moving onto Kazakh lands each year. Their settlements interfered with Kazakh nomadic routes, and tensions ran high between the two groups. The mounting frustration finally erupted in 1916, when the czar decreed that all his Central Asian subjects would assist Russia in its World War I effort. Kazakhs revolted and began attacking Russian military posts and settlements. The Russian soldiers and settlers responded with vicious attacks of their own. Some 300,000 Kazakhs fled east toward China to escape the escalating violence. Many froze or starved to death while crossing the rugged mountains that stood in their way.

A year later, Russia became caught up in a larger civil war. Czar Nicholas II was overthrown in February 1917, and Russia fell into four years of chaos as competing parties struggled for control of the country.

The civil war in Russia, coupled with the drain on resources caused by the First World War (1914–18), had a terrible effect on the economy of Kazakhstan. Making things even worse, in 1920–21 the harsh winter weather caused the deaths of almost half the livestock of Kazakhstan. During the resulting famine over the next few years, over a million people died on the steppes.

Russian settlers pose with their belongings on the steppes of Kazakhstan. In the late 19th and early 20th centuries, hundreds of thousands of Russians moved into Central Asia. The farms and communities the settlers established disrupted the traditional nomadic patterns of Kazakh life.

Kazakhstan and the Soviet Union

Kazakh leaders followed the events of the Russian Revolution with much interest, because they hoped the czar's downfall would lead to greater **autonomy** for Kazakhstan. They even went as far as to establish a political party, called Alash Orda, and a provisional Kazakh government. Alash Orda supported the communist Bolshevik movement during the civil war, with the expectation that the Bolsheviks would grant Kazakh autonomy if they won.

The Bolsheviks emerged victorious; by 1922 they had officially established the Union of Soviet Socialist Republics (U.S.S.R., or Soviet Union). Kazakhstan was initially part of the Kirgiz Autonomous Republic, formed in 1920, but in 1925 it was broken away and renamed the Kazakh Autonomous Soviet Socialist Republic. However, the Soviet leaders did not honor their promise of autonomy for Kazakhstan. The republic's leaders were chosen by the Soviets, and they did what they were told by their Russian masters.

When Joseph Stalin became the leader of the Soviet Union in 1924, he proved to be a harsher ruler than any Russian czar had ever been. In 1927 and 1928 he implemented a program that forced all peasant farmers and their herds onto government-owned farms. The Kazakhs opposed this program, known as collectivization. In protest, they slaughtered their livestock rather than turn the animals over to the government. However, this only resulted in another devastating famine. Over the next few years Kazakhstan's population dropped by 2 million people. Many died of starvation and disease; others fled the Soviet Union, crossing the mountains to settle in western China.

During the 1930s, Stalin systematically purged anyone he considered a threat to his power or to the communist cause. He believed that any person capable of independent thought posed a potential threat. In Kazakhstan, as in other parts of the Soviet Union, teachers, writers, politicians, and other intellectuals were either executed or deported to prison camps.

Stalin's deportation policies reached a peak during World War II (1939–45) when he banished entire populations he considered potentially disloyal. Kazakhstan became a favorite dumping ground for these unwanted peoples. In the early 1940s, large groups of uprooted Germans from the Volga River, Tatars, Chechens, and Koreans living in the Russian Far East were relocated to Kazakhstan.

World War II brought other changes to the steppes as well. Soviet industries were moved from western Russia, near the war zone, to the relative safety of Kazakhstan. For the first time, Kazakhs learned to work in factories. The republic became an important supplier of food, war goods, and manpower as the Soviet Union fought to defend its territory from the German invaders. The struggle gave Kazakhstan's increasingly diverse population a common goal and experience.

The particular demands of the war forced Stalin to relax his policies with regard to religion. Soviet officials had repressed the practice of Islam and other faiths within the U.S.S.R. Because religion unified people in a belief system other than communism, it was therefore considered a danger. Churches and mosques were razed during the 1920s and 1930s, and by 1935 only 20 public mosques remained open in Kazakhstan. However, Germany's 1941 invasion put the entire Soviet system at immediate risk, and to defend the country Stalin needed the help of the believers he had persecuted.

To reconcile with the Muslim community in Kazakhstan and other Central Asian lands, Stalin allowed mosques to reopen. He also created several government agencies that were supposedly dedicated to Islamic study. However, in reality these organizations were intended to monitor and control the Muslim population. Shortly after the war ended in 1945, the Soviet crackdown on religion resumed. Mosques were once again closed and Islam was officially classified as a cult.

After Stalin died in 1953, he was succeeded by Nikita Khrushchev, a leader who immediately sought to ease some of Stalin's oppressive policies. He initially called for tolerance of Islam, but this policy lasted only briefly. By 1958 the practice of Islam was once again officially forbidden, and Kazakhstan's Muslims, like those living elsewhere in the Soviet Union, returned to practicing their faith privately.

Khrushchev developed a special plan to boost Soviet agricultural production in a large region that included the Kazakh steppes. Under the Virgin Lands program, the steppes and southern Siberia would be transformed into prolific grain- and cotton-producing regions. Approximately 800,000 Russian farmers and engineers descended on the steppes, adding to the huge population of Russians that already lived there. By 1959, ethnic Kazakhs accounted for only 29 percent of the republic's population.

The Virgin Lands program set into motion many of the environmental difficulties that Kazakhstan faces today. The destruction of the Aral Sea, declining soil quality, and river and lake pollution can all be traced back to aggressive farming practices implemented during the 1950s. Ironically, these techniques never really turned Kazakhstan into the agricultural producer that Khrushchev had expected, even though it did become the Soviet Union's third-largest producer of grain. After achieving significant gains during the first few years of the Virgin Lands program, production fell as the fertile soil became depleted.

The man in charge of Kazakhstan's agricultural production during the mid-1950s was an official named Leonid Brezhnev. He became a powerful figure in the Communist Party, and in 1964, with the assistance of other Russian leaders, Brezhnev forced Krushchev from office and became the de facto ruler of Russia. After the tyranny of Joseph Stalin and the inconsistent policies of Nikita Khrushchev, Brezhnev wished to establish stability in the U.S.S.R. He also needed allies, as the **Cold War** between the Soviet Union and the United States was intensifying. To appease the

On April 12, 1961, Soviet cosmonaut Yuri Gagarin (1934–1968) became the first man in space. His Vostok 1 spacecraft was launched from the Baykonur complex in Kazakhstan. Vostok 1 completed an orbit of the earth before Gagarin parachuted safely to the ground.

U.S.S.R.'s Muslim population and curry favor with Muslim nations in the Middle East and elsewhere, Brezhnev eased restrictions against Islam. It was permitted to worship in mosques, observe holy days, and complete the *hajj*, although all religious activities took place under the watchful eye of the Soviet government.

Brezhnev achieved the stability he desired, and the Soviet Union settled into a period of relative calm during the 1970s and early 1980s. By this time, Kazakhstan was a fully integrated participant in the Soviet system. In a matter of decades, the pastoral wilderness of Kazakhstan had been transformed into a modernized republic and it was now an important contributor to a world superpower. Although some Kazakhstanis still wished for autonomy or outright freedom from Soviet rule, the majority of them enjoyed the security of military protection and Soviet social programs.

Brezhnev's stability came at a high cost, however. The Soviet Union stagnated and fell behind the United States in technology, economic growth, and military prowess. A Soviet invasion of Afghanistan in 1979 turned into a protracted guerilla war, costing many lives and draining valuable resources. When Leonid Brezhnev died in 1982, the Soviet Union was on the verge of losing the Cold War.

In 1985, after short periods of control by Yuri Andropov and Konstantin Chernenko, a reformer named Mikhail Gorbachev emerged as the Soviet leader. Gorbachev sought sweeping changes to modernize and restructure the failing economy of the Soviet Union. His policies also espoused greater social and political openness within the country. However, Islam remained repressed because Gorbachev felt that the religion's strict rules and practices could serve as an obstacle to modernization. Kazakhstanis distrusted his motives, and when Gorbachev installed an ethnic Russian at the head of Kazakhstan's government in 1986, people took to the streets in protest.

Although Kazakhstanis took issue with some of Gorbachev's policies, his reforms emboldened people throughout the Soviet Union. After decades of repression, Soviet citizens were invigorated by the opportunity to express themselves religiously and politically. Events spun from Gorbachev's control as the tides of change gained momentum. Mosques and churches were rebuilt and political groups were founded. The governments of the satellite republics, which had always been acquiescent, suddenly began making demands of Moscow. In 1990, the republic of Lithuania declared its independence. The Soviet Union was crumbling.

Era of Independence

Throughout 1991, the remaining Soviet republics broke away. By November of that year, all that remained were Kazakhstan and Russia. Kazakhstan had become more reliant on the Soviet Union than any other

This photograph was taken at one of the final meetings of Soviet leaders, September 3, 1991. Soviet reformer Mikhail Gorbachev is in the front row, second from left; seated with him are Kazakhstan's Communist Party leader Nazarbayev (far right) and Boris Yeltsin (center), who would go on to become president of Russia after the breakup of the Soviet Union in December.

republic, and feared the independence that so many others craved. When Kazakhstan finally declared its sovereignty in December 1991, it did so reluctantly.

The republic's top political leader at the time was Nursultan Nazarbayev, an ally of Gorbachev who had been appointed to power in 1989. In December 1991, he became Kazakhstan's first elected president. Kazakhstan joined a loose alliance of former Soviet republics called the

Commonwealth of Independent States (CIS). This move partly satisfied Nazarbayev's desire for a partnership between Kazakhstan and Russia, but he wanted to establish an even closer relationship. Such an agreement was never reached.

The first few years of independence saw much political experimentation in Kazakhstan. Some restrictions on the media were lifted, although no news story that found fault with the president could be reported. The government also permitted social and religious freedoms, as long as those actions did not stir ethnic tension.

Nazarbayev and others viewed the country's religious and ethnic diversity as potentially explosive. During the Soviet era, nearly all prejudices had been kept subdued by the threat of force, but that threat no longer existed. Therefore Kazakhstan's government could not show any tolerance for extremist groups that might incite cultural or religious fervor. These groups included a handful of Islamic organizations that advocated turning Kazakhstan into a **theocracy**, or religious state.

In 1993 Kazakhstan adopted its first constitution, and in 1994 the country's first multiparty legislative elections were held. However, the elections were not truly democratic. Government-endorsed candidates were given unfair advantages, such as better media coverage, while opposition candidates struggled just to get their names on the ballot. When the votes were counted, roughly 90 percent of the winners were those with close ties to the Nazarbayev government.

Despite the new legislature's makeup, it proved to be an independent-minded group. Nazarbayev had hoped for a compliant body that would rubber-stamp all his initiatives. Instead, the parliament disagreed with him on many issues, especially his fast-paced plan for economic reform. Some legislators complained that Nazarbayev was moving toward privatization too quickly, thus jeopardizing the fragile Kazakh economy. The general public shared their belief.

Kazakhstan's judges did not have the same independent spirit as its legislators. In early 1995, the constitutional court unexpectedly ruled that the results of the previous year's legislative election were invalid. President Nazarbayev immediately dissolved parliament and sent the legislators home. Rumors swirled that Nazarbayev had influenced the court's decision, and disgruntled legislators called for an international inquiry. The court's ruling stood, however, and Nazarbayev took complete control of the government until new elections could be held.

Nazarbayev used the opportunity to strengthen his power. He first ordered a national referendum to determine if his term as president should be extended until the year 2000. The voters approved this measure, and Nazarbayev next moved to have the national constitution revised. The new constitution greatly expanded presidential authority, scaled back the role of the legislature, and gave the president the power to dismiss the assembly at will. To guarantee future cooperation from that body, Nazarbayev stocked the 1996 parliamentary elections with candidates of his choosing.

In 1997, Nazarbayev took the unusual and expensive step of transferring the nation's capital to another city. The government's headquarters moved from Almaty in the southeast to the tiny city of Aqmola (also spelled *Akmola*) in north-central Kazakhstan. Aqmola was renamed Astana, which literally means "capital city" in Kazakh. Government officials cited Almaty's poor road network and susceptibility to earthquakes as reasons for the move. However, most foreign analysts believe the true reason was to give the government closer proximity to Kazakhstan's northern provinces.

Although Nazarbayev was not scheduled to stand for reelection until early 2000, in late 1998 the date of the election was unexpectedly moved up to January 1999. Nazarbayev's opponents had little chance to prepare, and the election was a landslide victory in his favor.

Parliamentary elections were held in the fall of 1999, and Nazarbayev supporters captured 80 percent of the vote. However, international observers reported that the elections did not meet democratic standards.

The same people who seized political power in the 1990s also amassed huge personal fortunes. Nazarbayev helped his friends and family members to prosper financially. They took ownership of newly privatized companies, received illicit payments from foreign oil companies, and accepted bribes for lucrative government contracts. As these favors were being exchanged, average Kazakhstanis were struggling with skyrocketing inflation and severe unemployment.

Nazarbayev also used family ties to secure his control of the nation. At the start of the new millennium, close relatives occupied vital positions in

Nazarbayev listens to his country's national anthem during his inauguration ceremony, January 20, 1999. Ten days earlier, he won reelection as president with nearly 82 percent of the vote; opponents claimed that the balloting had been rigged in his favor.

government, the media, the military, and the oil industry. Other relatives of the president held key jobs in the mining and metallurgy sectors, as well as in companies involved with the production of food, tobacco, and alcohol. The Nazarbayev family and its associates were believed to be skimming profits from virtually every segment of Kazakhstan's economy. Yet throughout this period, the president waged a high-profile campaign against government corruption at the local level.

After a decade of independence, Kazakhstan seemed to have gained confidence in itself. No longer did it seek protection from Russia. Foreign countries were competing for a share of Kazakhstan's natural resources, and they provided the young nation with financial aid and technology. The disruptive transitions of privatization were nearly complete. In 2000 the European Union officially recognized Kazakhstan as having a free-market economy, and in 2002 the United States did the same.

The outlook for average citizens also gradually improved. By 2005 some benefits from the booming petroleum industry were finally trickling down to the underprivileged. Inflation and unemployment became more manageable. The danger of ethnic conflict continued to loom, but there were no signs of it worsening. While Kazakhstanis detested the government's rampant corruption, most cynically accepted it as part of life.

Despite the economic progress that has been made, many Kazakhstanis are still dissatisfied. The gap between rich and poor continues to widen. The government is unable to deliver basic services, such as health care and police protection, to some areas. Organized crime has flourished. Muslim extremists from surrounding nations have made inroads in the country's south. This myriad of political and economic shortcomings makes Kazakhstan a potential recruiting ground for terrorist groups.

Oil workers service an oil well located about 124 miles (200 km) north of Kyzylorda. Petroleum is the backbone of Kazakhstan's economy, and today the country produces about a million barrels of oil each day.

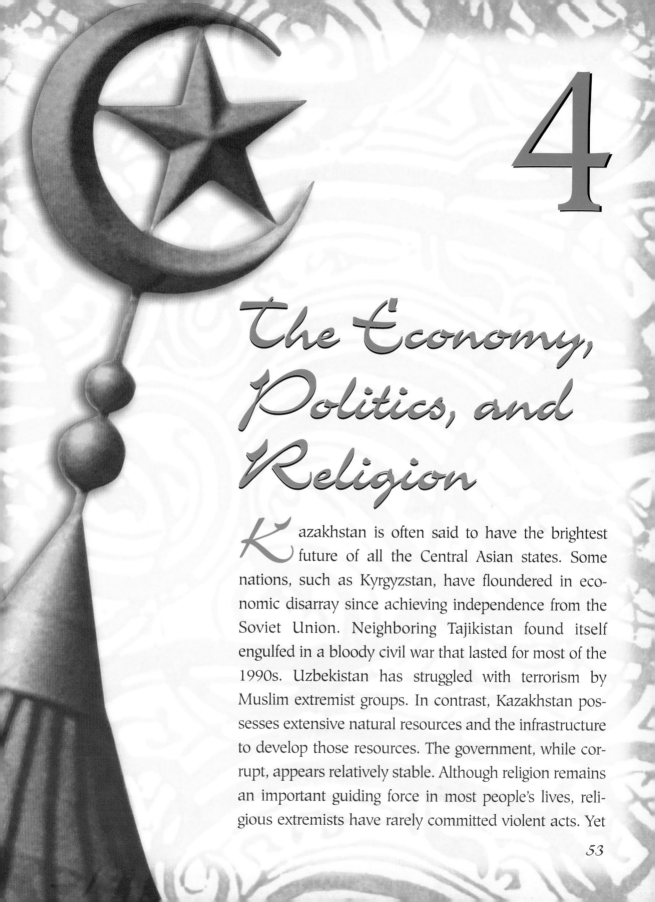

4

The Economy, Politics, and Religion

*K*azakhstan is often said to have the brightest future of all the Central Asian states. Some nations, such as Kyrgyzstan, have floundered in economic disarray since achieving independence from the Soviet Union. Neighboring Tajikistan found itself engulfed in a bloody civil war that lasted for most of the 1990s. Uzbekistan has struggled with terrorism by Muslim extremist groups. In contrast, Kazakhstan possesses extensive natural resources and the infrastructure to develop those resources. The government, while corrupt, appears relatively stable. Although religion remains an important guiding force in most people's lives, religious extremists have rarely committed violent acts. Yet

53

the situation in Kazakhstan appears favorable only when compared to that of its troubled neighbors. Many bold steps will need to be taken before the young republic can reach its true potential.

The Economy

The key to Kazakhstan's economy is petroleum. During the Soviet era, Kazakhstan was recognized as a likely location of massive oil reserves. However, Siberia remained the Soviet Union's primary petroleum producer and Kazakhstan's reserves went largely untapped.

Under the economic reforms instituted by Mikhail Gorbachev in the 1980s, Kazakhstan was permitted for the first time to accept offers from foreign oil companies for drilling rights. The American company Chevron was the first to strike a deal in Kazakhstan. After several years of negotiations, Chevron began developing the gigantic Tengiz oil field in the country's western region. A pipeline now carries Tengiz oil through Russia and to the Black Sea for shipment around the world. Other deals soon followed, and today Kazakhstan produces roughly a million barrels of oil per day.

The most remarkable aspect of Kazakhstan's petroleum industry is its potential for future growth. Numerous oil fields, both on land and under the Caspian Sea, are currently being prepared for drilling. As those fields become active, the country's oil production is expected to climb to 1.6 million barrels per day by 2010, and to 2 million barrels per day by 2015. The government has set a long-term goal of becoming one of the top five oil-producing nations in the world.

The mining of various metal and chemical deposits is also important to Kazakhstan's economy. However, the mining industry is plagued by numerous legal disputes that slow productivity. Foreign investors have in the past quarreled with Kazakhstan's government over ownership rights for several mines. In 2000, the government resolved some of these disputes but others remain. Kazakhstan's steel industry is frequently accused of unfair trading practices. The United States, China, and other nations have periodically imposed tariffs against Kazakhstan's steel as a result. Despite the sanctions, Kazakhstan still exports about 4 million tons (3.6 million metric tons) of steel annually.

Agriculture is another important sector for trade. Each year, Kazakhstan exports large quantities of wheat to Russia, China, Iran, and its Central Asian neighbors. Other crops include barley, cotton, and rice, as well as livestock-related products such as dairy goods, leather, meat, and wool. Kazakhstan typically has a significant trade surplus each year.

Russia continues to be the nation's largest trading partner, but China, Germany, Italy, and the United States also account for considerable trade.

This satellite image of the Turgayskaya Oblast in central Kazakhstan shows how agricultural activities and mining occur side by side in the country. The large square shapes are fields of spring wheat, one of the cereal grains that grow well in the country's cold, dry climate. The colorful irregular patterns on the left are surface-mining operations, probably for the extraction of bauxite or asbestos; water has accumulated in the mines to form small lakes.

The U.S. imports petroleum and metals from Kazakhstan while sending the country aircraft, oil drilling equipment, and medical supplies. U.S. corporations have invested roughly $7 billion in Kazakhstan since 1993. The majority of this investment comes from oil companies, but American firms also have major interests in Kazakh agriculture and financial services. Companies from many other nations operate in Kazakhstan as well.

Huge sums of foreign capital flowing into the country have prompted Kazakhstan's government to take an active role in fighting inflation. In recent years, inflation has been contained to an annual rate of about 6 percent. The government's ability to limit inflation has impressed the world financial community. Additionally, Kazakhstan's banking system has been described as the most developed in Central Asia. President Nazarbayev now talks of Kazakhstan becoming a major economic power in both Europe and Asia.

The Effect of Economic Reforms

Only two decades ago the country was mired in the failing Soviet economy. The defunct Soviet economic system left Kazakhstan with a decaying infrastructure and a dependence on Russia for many goods and services. Additionally, many ethnic Russians who held high-level industrial jobs throughout Kazakhstan returned to their native homeland after 1991, creating a management crisis. Economic productivity virtually ground to a halt and unemployment rates soared.

Despite the financial devastation, or perhaps because of it, the government pressed ahead with a rapid privatization program. By 1999, over 75 percent of the economy was in the hands of business owners and capitalists. The privatization process was rife with corruption, and Nazarbayev's relatives and associates took ownership of Kazakhstan's largest and most profitable companies. The government retained partial ownership of lucrative industries such as oil and natural gas production, railroads, and telecommunications.

The Economy of Kazakhstan

Gross Domestic Product (GDP*): $105.3 billion
GDP per capita: $7,000
Inflation: 6.2%
Natural resources: major deposits of petroleum, natural gas, coal, iron ore, manganese, chrome ore, nickel, cobalt, copper, molybdenum, lead, zinc, bauxite, gold, uranium
Industry (35.4% of GDP): oil, coal, iron ore, manganese, chromite, lead, zinc, copper, titanium, bauxite, gold, silver, phosphates, sulfur, iron and steel, tractors and other agricultural machinery, electric motors, construction materials (2002 est.)
Agriculture (7.9% of GDP): grain (mostly spring wheat), cotton, livestock (2002 est.)
Services (56.7% of GDP): government, financial services, tourism (2002 est.)
Foreign trade:
  Imports: $8.621 billion—machinery and equipment, metal products, foodstuffs
  Exports: $12.72 billion—oil and oil products, ferrous metals, chemicals, machinery, grain, wool, meat, coal
Currency exchange rate (2004): U.S. $1 = 135.67 Kazakh tenges

*GDP is the total value of goods and services produced in a year.
All figures are 2003 estimates unless otherwise noted.
Source: CIA World Factbook, 2004; bloomberg.com.

The reformed economy began to grow at a rate of 10 to 15 percent annually. However, much of the growth came in sectors still controlled by the government, especially the petroleum industry. The general populace received little benefit from these gains. The Nazarbayev regime claimed that unemployment dropped to 13 percent in 2000, and fell again to 8 percent in 2002, but most economists doubted the accuracy of these figures.

Initially, the government used its newfound wealth for debt repayment and other projects. In 2000, Kazakhstan became the first former Soviet republic to repay loans received from the International Monetary Fund (IMF) at the time of independence. The loans, which totaled $400 million, were repaid seven years early. The government also invested heavily in construction of the new capital in Astana. Many people in Kazakhstan and the international community questioned the decision to build a new capital instead of addressing the country's numerous social problems.

More recently, the government has shown greater compassion for its citizens. In 2002, more than a quarter of a billion dollars was set aside to improve the country's crumbling road network. In 2003, funding for the country's meager health care system was nearly doubled. A portion of the petroleum revenue is now placed in a National Oil Fund dedicated to improving the quality of life for future generations. The fund's value currently exceeds $3 billion. Critics applaud these measures but contend that far more must be done.

In 2003, Kazakhstan's Land Law went into effect. The legislation permitted private ownership of farmland and commercial buildings. Previously, farmers and businessmen were required to lease property from the government. Private land ownership is an important step toward economic prosperity and social equity in Kazakhstan.

Government and Politics

Under Soviet rule, Kazakhstan's government was modeled after, and subservient to, the central government in Moscow. The republic's political leader was the first secretary of the Communist Party of Kazakhstan, a position that Nazarbayev was appointed to in 1989. In 1990 the title was changed to president, but it remained an appointed instead of an elected position. The legislature during this period was known as the Supreme Soviet.

Following independence, the legislature was renamed the Supreme Kenges and the presidency became an elected position. In 1993, the country's first constitution established a unicameral, or single-chamber, legislature consisting of 177 elected members.

Revisions to the constitution in 1995 split the legislature into two chambers, making it bicameral. The upper chamber is the Senate, which has 39 seats. Seven senators are appointed by the president, and the other 32 are elected. Senators serve for six years at a time. The lower chamber is called the **Majilis**, which means "assembly," and it has 77 seats. Majilis members serve five-year terms and all are elected.

Today's legislature wields far less authority than did the original parliament. The constitutional amendments of 1995 made the office of the president extremely powerful. The president may dissolve the legislature; make constitutional amendments; schedule a referendum; and make appointments to powerful government positions without the legislature's review. The constitution states that presidential elections will be held every seven years; however, as the surprise election in January 1999 demonstrated, the incumbent president may reschedule elections at his discretion.

The president appoints a prime minister, who oversees the daily activities of the government. In June 2003, President Nazarbayev appointed Daniyal Akhmetov as prime minister. The president also has a cabinet of ministers to advise him on important matters. Each of the 18 ministers heads a department of government such as foreign affairs, environmental protection, and finance.

Two courts sit atop Kazakhstan's judicial system: the Supreme Court and the Constitutional Council (formerly the Constitutional Court). The Supreme Court has 44 judges, who are appointed for life by the president. The Constitutional Council, whose job is to interpret the constitution

Kazakhstan's Prime Minister Daniyal Akhmetov (right) meets Chinese Premier Wen Jiabao during trade talks in Beijing. In Kazakhstan's government the prime minister is appointed by the president to oversee the daily activities of the government's 18 ministers.

when challenges arise, has seven judges. The president appoints three of these judges; the remaining four are appointed by the legislature. The president also has the right to veto Constitutional Council decisions.

The government of Kazakhstan likes to boast that the country has 19 political parties. However, this statement is somewhat misleading because there are only a handful of opposition parties and they have little influence. In 2002, a law was passed requiring parties to have at least 50,000 members before they could be registered. By March 2004, only nine parties met the requirement. Opposition leaders have been the victims of government harassment, and in some cases, false arrest.

Under constitutional law, the president is not permitted to have any party affiliation. However, this rule does not reflect actual practices within the country. President Nazarbayev is closely tied to the Otan (Fatherland) Party, which currently controls the legislature. He also draws heavy support from the many independent members of parliament.

Kazakhstan is divided into 14 **oblasts**, or provinces, and three major city districts—Almaty, Astana, and Baykonur. The oblasts consist of large swaths of sparsely populated land. Each oblast has a governing council, called a *maslikhat*, which has a council leader called an *akim*. The president exercises tight control over the oblasts, and appoints the *akim* himself. In 1997, the boundaries of the oblasts were redrawn so that the Russian-dominated northern oblasts, which President Nazarbayev feared had grown too independent, included more ethnic Kazakhs.

The government is extremely sensitive to criticism from foreign countries. In recent years, programs have been implemented to show the world that Kazakhstan is committed to democracy. Government organizations were created to address human rights violations, election reform, and censorship. The government of Kazakhstan hires public relation firms all over the world to enhance its image.

In 2001, the government experimented with the elections of *akims* in certain regions. Three years later, it claimed the results were still being analyzed to determine if local elections could be expanded to all regions. When foreign leaders have suggested that such reforms could move at a faster pace, Nazarbayev has replied that Kazakhstan is not yet ready for full democracy.

Nazarbayev has been the driving force in Kazakh politics since he first came to power in 1989. Since independence, he has set Kazakhstan's path and is chiefly responsible for the nation that exists today. Born in 1940 in a small village near Almaty, Nazarbayev first attended technical college before going to work at a metallurgy plant. It was here that he became interested in politics. After 10 years of operating a blast furnace, he left the plant to work full-time for the Communist Party. By age 44, he occupied a prominent position in Kazakh government, and five years later he was named its head.

Rewarding loyalty has always been the cornerstone of Nazarbayev's success. By making his supporters the wealthiest and most powerful people in Kazakhstan, the president is virtually assured of remaining in office for as long as he wishes. When the time does come for him to step down, many believe that a close relative will succeed him. Nazarbayev's daughters and

The light blue background of Kazakhstan's flag represents the endless sky; in the center, a stylized eagle flies beneath a golden sun shooting 32 rays. An ornamental border runs from top to bottom on the hoist side of the flag.

sons-in-law maintain high-profile careers in government and industry. Political observers strongly suspect that at least one of these family members is being groomed for the presidency.

President Nazarbayev is certainly an authoritarian leader, but he is not a dictator. Many of Kazakhstan's neighbors, particularly Turkmenistan and Uzbekistan, live under far more oppressive regimes. Kazakh leaders are increasingly concerned that civil unrest in those nations will spill over into Kazakhstan. In recent years, the government has more than tripled defense spending in order to protect its borders.

Role of Islam

Throughout the 1990s, Central Asia garnered much attention from the international community due to its massive oil reserves. Following the terrorist attacks in the United States on September 11, 2001, Central Asia took on a new importance. The region's proximity to Afghanistan, Iraq, and Iran, combined with its high Muslim population, thrust it into the world spotlight. While Kazakhstan is generally considered the least Muslim state in the region, the importance of Islam cannot be understated.

The word *Islam* is derived from an Arabic verb that means "to submit," and devout Muslims believe that through their religious practices they are submitting to the will of God. Islam originated on the Arabian Peninsula during the seventh century A.D., when a man named Muhammad (ca. 570–632) began teaching that there was a single god, called Allah, and that He wanted all people to obey and worship Him. Muhammad's teachings of an omnipotent, merciful God who loves all Muslims equally appealed to people of every social class and race. Coupled with Arab military prowess, the religion quickly spread as far west as Spain and North Africa and as far east as India and China.

Islam's rapid expansion included the southernmost fringes of Central Asia, but not the Kazakhstan region. The nomads of the steppes did not fully accept the new faith until the 12th century, when Muslim missionaries arrived in the region. Until this time, the nomads had followed animist belief systems, which usually involved the worship of spirits that were found in animals and nature.

Later missionaries to the region brought a form of the religion called **Sufism**, which stresses a simple, pious life in order to achieve direct and personal communication with God. Sufis are more concerned with the spiritual aspects of Islam than its strict social requirements. They also preach tolerance toward other beliefs. The Sufis' personal approach to Islam appealed to the independent-minded Kazakhs, and this helped the religion gain wider acceptance throughout the steppes.

The Russians, who began arriving in the 19th century, practiced Christianity as members of the Russian Orthodox Church. Soviet resettlement programs during the 20th century also brought people of other Christian denominations, such as Lutherans and Roman Catholics. None of these groups significantly influenced the ethnic Kazakhs, however, who continued to practice their informal version of Islam.

During most of the Soviet era, Kazakh Muslims were forced to worship secretly. Prayer gatherings and religious classes were held in private homes, typically at night. Makeshift mosques opened in forgotten graveyards. Islamic scholars, or **mullahs**, quietly traveled among communities to perform religious rites. Local government officials, who were often Muslims themselves, pretended to be unaware of such activities.

The Soviet Union's decline in the late 1980s and early 1990s allowed Muslims to once again practice their faith openly. The number of mosques operating in Kazakhstan skyrocketed. Before long, a new mosque was opening nearly every day. Sufi shrines were restored or rebuilt and once again became hubs for social activities.

Islamic extremism also sprouted up in Central Asia during this period. In the early 1980s, many young men from the region were conscripted to serve with the Soviet army in Afghanistan. These men resented being forced to fight the Afghans, who were fellow Muslims. Upon returning to Central Asia, they told stories of bravery shown by Afghan Muslims in resisting the Soviet invasion. Afghan efforts to overthrow the Soviet-backed secular government during the country's civil war (1979–89) and establish an Islamic state inspired some Muslims in Central Asia to try to do the same. Islamic extremist groups became active all across the region, including in Kazakhstan. However, most of these organizations originated in neighboring countries. Their attempts to recruit Kazakhstani members succeeded only in the extreme south, near the border with Uzbekistan.

From the very beginning, the secular government of independent Kazakhstan viewed religious extremism as a threat. At the time of independence, the numbers of Muslims and Christians living in Kazakhstan were virtually equal. The parity between two major religions made Kazakhstan unique among the former Soviet republics of Central Asia, most of which were predominately Muslim. Kazakhstan's leaders felt it necessary to establish a truly secular government that favored neither Christians nor Muslims. Therefore, Islamic law did not play a role in the development of Kazakhstan's legal system as it did in the other newly independent states.

Upon gaining independence, most Kazakhstanis considered religion a personal matter that should remain separate from government and politics. That belief has gradually started to change. Russian Christians are steadily migrating out of the country, thus making Islam the dominant religion. Today, the population of Kazakhstan is estimated to be 47 percent Muslim and 44 percent Russian Orthodox (the remaining 9 percent represent various other belief systems). In the coming years, the proportion of Muslims is expected to continue increasing.

In addition to this major population change, the nature of Islam in Kazakhstan is changing. Beginning in the 1990s, some Kazakh Muslims

A new mosque is under construction in Astana. Since Kazakhstan became independent, the practice of Islam has grown more widespread, although the religion's influence over daily life remains limited.

exercised their newfound freedom to travel abroad and journeyed to the Middle East as students. They returned educated in the ways of traditional Islam. Also at this time, waves of missionaries and literature arrived from the Middle East urging Central Asians to adopt traditional Islamic practices. Attitudes began to shift. A 1997 survey of Kazakh Muslims, conducted by the U.S. Information Agency, found that 61 percent felt there should be a place for religion in the state's affairs.

The Nazarbayev regime has felt increasingly threatened by the influence of foreign religious scholars. In 1998, missionaries from Pakistan,

Egypt, Sudan, and Jordan were arrested for their activities and deported. The government stepped up its efforts in 1999 after terrorist bombings rocked Uzbekistan's capital of Tashkent, just miles from the Kazakh border. In 2000, the government started recalling citizens who were studying abroad at certain Islamic schools, and since 2001 Kazakhstan has been an ardent supporter of the U.S.-led war on terrorism.

Many antiterrorism experts believe that Kazakhstan's government has inadvertently created an ideal environment for Islamic extremism. They say that instead of focusing on foreign influences, the Nazarbayev regime should examine its own domestic policies. Extremist groups tend to flourish in poverty-stricken societies that are ruled by a wealthy and selfish elite. It is no coincidence that southern Kazakhstan is both the poorest region in the country and also the most prone to Islamic extremism. The government's best strategy against terrorism may be to concentrate more on improving the welfare of its citizens.

A Kazakh hunter lets his golden eagle fly during a hunting competition in the Elan Tau region. The use of trained eagles to hunt for small animals is an ancient Kazakh tradition.

5

the People

T he concept of nationality is relatively new to the people of Central Asia. For centuries, inhabitants of the region based their self-identity on factors such as religion or clan membership. The term *nation* was foreign to these people, particularly to the nomads of the Kazakh steppes. Political boundaries did not even exist in Central Asia until Soviet leaders established them in the 1920s.

Today, the borders often hold little more meaning than they did over 80 years ago. Kazakhstanis generally do not view themselves as citizens of Kazakhstan. To them, Kazakhstan just happens to be the place where they live. They put far more importance on their ethnic and religious background. The government of Kazakhstan, like the Soviet government before it, has attempted to persuade citizens that they are a single people with a common heritage.

Those efforts have largely failed. Although Kazakhstan's cultural diversity is a legacy of the former Soviet Union, Kazakhstanis are a less diverse people now than they were under Soviet rule. Independence triggered a series of population shifts that are still in motion today. Some ethnic groups have emigrated from Kazakhstan while others have experienced population growth. As a result, the nation's ethnic composition is significantly different from what it was just two decades ago.

Ethnic Composition

Four out of every five Kazakhstanis are either Russian or Kazakh. For most of the 20th century, Russians were the dominant group. They occupied important positions in government and industry, while the Kazakhs were often treated like second-class citizens.

The relationship changed after Kazakhstan declared its independence from the Soviet Union in 1991. Ethnic Kazakhs began asserting themselves politically. Statues of Soviet heroes were torn down, and Russian-named city streets were given new Kazakh names. The silent, grudging respect that had always been afforded to ethnic Russians was suddenly gone. In its place was Kazakh pride and resentment.

With the rise in Kazakh influence, President Nazarbayev feared a revolt from the Russian-dominated north. He wanted the Russians to feel a part of the new nation, and so granted citizenship to all residents regardless of their ethnic background.

Despite the assurances, many Russians feared that now it was their turn to be discriminated against. They did not wish to be citizens of a Kazakh-run state. Some simply packed their belongings and departed for Russia. By 1994, tens of thousands of ethnic Russians were leaving the country each year. In *Kazakhstan: Unfulfilled Promise*, Martha Brill Olcott writes that 1.5 million Russians left Kazakhstan for Russia from 1992 to 2000. Those who remained demanded dual citizenship, meaning that they would be legal citizens of both Kazakhstan and Russia at the same time. Others spoke of uniting northern Kazakhstan with Russia.

In an effort to pacify the Russian population, Nazarbayev negotiated with Russian president Boris Yeltsin to make it easier for Kazakhstanis to transfer their citizenship to Russia if they so desired. Ethnic Russians who felt they were being treated unfairly in Kazakhstan would always have the option of moving to Russia without much difficulty. While the policy did not fully satisfy Kazakhstan's Russians, it provided them with a greater sense of security and ended most calls for dual citizenship, although the issue still surfaces occasionally in public debates.

As the Russian population declined, the ethnic Kazakh population increased. In 1989, Kazakhs accounted for 40 percent of the nation's population and Russians accounted for 37 percent. By 1999, Kazakhs made up 53 percent of the population while Russians made up only 30 percent.

Russian emigration was primarily responsible for the shift, but there were other factors as well. Kazakhs observe the Middle Eastern tradition of having large families, while Russian families typically have fewer children. In 1999, a group of Kazakh businessmen sought to encourage this trend by offering cash bonuses to the parents of newborns. The offer was officially open to all Kazakhstanis, but everyone knew it favored ethnic Kazakhs.

In addition to Russians, large numbers of ethnic Germans left Kazakhstan after the country gained its independence. In 1989, nearly a million ethnic Germans lived in the country. Joseph Stalin had deported them from western Russia during World War II because he doubted their loyalty to the Soviet Union. The Federal Republic of Germany—reunited in 1989–90 after the fall of the Berlin Wall—was anxious to have these people back and during the 1990s offered them financial incentives to return. Within a decade, only about 350,000 Germans remained in Kazakhstan. Ethnic Ukrainians followed a similar pattern, although in

German children (known as Volga Germans) pay attention during a geography class in Ilitzki, Kazakhstan, December 1991. The Volga Germans were ethnic Germans who lived for centuries along the Volga River in western Russia, where they maintained German culture, language, traditions, and religions. During World War II, as the armies of Nazi Germany invaded Russia, Soviet leader Joseph Stalin became concerned that the Volga Germans would collaborate with the Nazis. He ordered them to be relocated to concentration camps in the eastern Soviet Union; after the war, the survivors settled in Kazakhstan, Siberia, and the Ural Mountains. Many of the Volga Germans left Kazakhstan during the 1990s.

smaller numbers because they were not given any financial motivation to emigrate.

Kazakh repatriation has been another factor in changing the population demographics. Initially, the government of Kazakhstan encouraged the roughly 4 million ethnic Kazakhs living outside the country—primarily the descendants of those who fled Kazakhstan during the early years of Soviet rule—to return home. These people reside in China, Mongolia,

Uzbekistan, and elsewhere. In the mid-1990s, the government helped 60,000 Kazakhs move from Mongolia to eastern Kazakhstan. However, repatriating ethnic Kazakhs from other nations proved to be a difficult undertaking. The Mongolian Kazakhs retained the nomadic lifestyle of their ancestors and, as a result, had little in common with modern-day Kazakhstanis. The differences demonstrated just how much Kazakhstan's culture had changed under the Soviets. Today, the government does not actively attempt to repatriate Kazakhs from foreign countries.

Culture Clashes

The population shift in favor of Kazakhs made Nazarbayev less concerned about upsetting his Russian citizens. As a result, efforts to incorporate Kazakh traditions into society were met with less government resistance. The drive to make Kazakh the nation's official language is a highly controversial example.

For nearly 70 years, Russian was the dominant language in Kazakhstan. Russian was taught in schools, spoken at work, and broadcast over the airwaves. Ethnic Kazakhs continued to speak their native language at home, but were forced to use Russian in public. Ethnic Russians, on the other hand, were not required to learn Kazakh.

In the years following independence, language came to exemplify the social tension between Russians and Kazakhs. A number of political groups proposed adopting Kazakh as the official state language. They argued that the majority of the population should not be forced to speak a foreign tongue. Russians viewed the proposal as yet another attempt to discriminate against them. In 1993, Kazakh was named the country's official language, but the use of Russian was not prohibited. Instead, Russian would continue to be spoken in public settings while Kazakh was gradually introduced. Additionally, the constitution recognized Russian as the language of international communication.

The conversion from Russian to Kazakh as a primary language has not gone as smoothly as hoped. A considerable segment of the population is resisting the change, including most Russians and even some ethnic Kazakhs. The country's 1999 census revealed that 75 percent of the population speaks Russian fluently, but only 64 percent speaks Kazakh. While some Kazakhstanis are clearly fluent in both tongues, language continues to be a social barrier for many.

Government officials have sought to increase the percentage of Kazakh-speakers by mandating its use in the nation's educational system. However, 70 years of Soviet repression has made Kazakh something of an outdated language. No Kazakh words exist to describe products of modern science and technology. In addition, most existing textbooks are written in Russian and some regions have a shortage of qualified Kazakh-speaking teachers. As recently as 1999, 72 percent of college students were still being taught in Russian. English has become a popular compromise. Students are learning English with the hope of studying abroad, while business executives are learning it in order to build international relationships.

The language issue does not merely divide ethnic Russians and Kazakhs; it also divides Kazakhs among themselves. Each of the three hordes that comprise the ethnic Kazakh population has a different linguistic background. The Great Horde, which hails from southeastern Kazakhstan, has the largest number of Kazakh-speakers. The Middle Horde, which originated in the central steppes, and the Little Horde of the west both have greater concentrations of Russian-speakers. Naturally, the Great Horde has more to gain by making Kazakh the national language.

Rivalries between the three hordes, or *zhuzes* as they are known in Kazakh, date back for centuries. In nomadic times, the three groups competed for grazing lands, foreign trade, and political influence. The rivalries diminished during the periods of Russian and Soviet rule, but did not

The People of Kazakhstan

Population: 16,763,795
Ethnic groups: Kazakh 53.4%, Russian 30%, Ukrainian
3.7%, Uzbek 2.5%, German 2.4%, Uygur 1.4%, other
6.6% (1999 census)
Religions: Muslim 47%, Russian Orthodox 44%, Protestant
2%, other 7%
Age structure:
  0–14 years: 24.4%
  15–64 years: 68%
  65 years and over: 7.6%
Population growth rate: 0.26%
Birth rate: 15.52 births/1,000 population
Infant mortality rate: 30.54 deaths/1,000 live births
Death rate: 9.59 deaths/1,000 population
Life expectancy at birth:
  total population: 66.07 years
  male: 60.72 years
  female: 71.73 years
Total fertility rate: 1.9 children born/woman
Literacy: 98.4% (1999 est.)

All figures are 2004 estimates unless otherwise noted.
Source: Adapted from CIA World Factbook, 2004.

disappear. Kazakhs take great pride in knowing their family history. A Kazakh maxim says, "He is a fool who has forgotten what became of his ancestry seven generations before him and who does not care what will become of his progeny seven generations after him."

Clan rivalries were renewed once it became clear that the Soviet Union would disintegrate. Each horde jockeyed for power in the newly independent state. The Great Horde won out, largely because the new president was a member. However, Nazarbayev's early political career was aided by the political influence of his wife's Middle Horde family. Marriage is one method of developing political alliances in Central Asia. In 1998, the Nazarbayevs' youngest daughter married the oldest son of Kyrgyzstan's president. The wedding was celebrated as a sign of unity between the two nations. However, the marriage was short-lived, and the divorce between the presidents' children stood as a reminder that good diplomacy between Kazakhstan and its neighbors depends on more than inter-family unions.

Although clan and family loyalties are crucial elements in ethnic Kazakh culture, they also serve as obstacles in Kazakhstan's society as a whole. Russians and other ethnic groups continue to be labeled as outsiders, even if they have lived their entire lives in Kazakhstan. Different religious beliefs between Russians and Kazakhs merely reinforce these attitudes.

Religious Practices

Kazakhstan has a Muslim community of approximately 8 million people, most of whom belong to the Sunni branch of the faith. Sunnis make up more than 80 percent of the worldwide Muslim community, and they believe that they are following the path of submission to God's will established by Muhammad and his companions. However, Muslims in Kazakhstan do not observe the strict moral codes often found in other Islamic societies. For example, the consumption of alcohol is permitted, and Kazakh women are not required to veil their faces in public.

There are five important teachings on which Islam is based, known as the five pillars. The first pillar of Islam is the profession of faith, a declaration of belief in God. A Muslim acknowledges his or her belief by reciting the statement "There is no god but Allah, and Muhammad is His prophet." The words are often repeated during prayer—the second pillar of Islam. Muslims are required to pray on five occasions during the day—at dawn, noon, midafternoon, sunset, and in the evening. The third pillar of Islam, almsgiving or charity, involves providing assistance for the poor and needy. The fourth pillar is observance of the holy month of Ramadan, the ninth month of the Islamic lunar calendar. During Ramadan, able-bodied Muslims must refrain from eating or drinking between sunup and sundown. Finally, the fifth pillar of Islam requires adult Muslims to make a pilgrimage to the holy city of Mecca at least once during their lifetimes, if they are physically and financially able to do so.

Although Kazakhstani Muslims, like Muslims in other parts of the world, are expected to keep the five pillars of Islam, surveys have shown that many Kazakhs do not know these basic beliefs of their religion. When the U.S. Information Agency interviewed 2,000 Kazakhstani adults in 1997, for example, only 48 percent of those who identified themselves as

Kazakhs pray before a Nauryz celebration meal in the village of Berektas. Nauryz is a traditional Central Asian holiday that marks the first day of spring.

Muslims could name a single pillar of Islam. However, in recent years religion has played a greater role in daily life, and as a result many more Kazakhstani Muslims now understand the tenets of Islam.

Each Muslim is expected to struggle against the temptations of evil in order to become a better person. The Prophet Muhammad described *jihad* as a spiritual struggle within each person. Muslims must also struggle against what they perceive as the ignorance of non-Muslims by teaching them the ways of Islam. However, some Muslim extremists define jihad as a "holy war" against nonbelievers and use it as justification for violence. Extremist groups typically want to impose strict Islamic law as a way to control society. Although most Muslims reject these views, Islamic extremists have more followers today than they did a decade ago. In Kazakhstan, extremism is limited to small pockets in the south.

Some of the 5 million ethnic Russians living in Kazakhstan are Muslim, but most belong to the Russian Orthodox Christian Church. The Russian Orthodox church was established in the 10th century. It was an offshoot of the Orthodox Christian church that developed in the Eastern half of the Roman Empire.

Christianity is based on the teachings of Jesus, a Jewish man who lived in Judea (part of the modern state of Israel). Jesus claimed to be the messiah, the Son of God, and preached a message of repentance and humility. His teachings offended devout Jews, and they conspired with Roman authorities to have him arrested, tortured, and executed by being nailed to a cross around the year A.D. 29. His followers, however, believed that Jesus' death had been necessary to save mankind from its sins, and reported that He had risen from the dead and would return one day to judge all mankind. Early Christian missionaries like Paul, Peter, Luke, Andrew, Bartholomew, and others began to preach this "Good News" throughout Judea, then spread the message into the Roman provinces of Asia, Africa, and Europe.

Initially, Christianity was a religion that appealed primarily to slaves, women, or people of the lower classes, and its followers were periodically persecuted by Roman authorities. The Roman Emperor Constantine legalized Christianity, however, and by the time of his death in 337 it was the de facto religion of the empire.

After 395 the Roman Empire became permanently divided into eastern and western halves. The two halves met separate fates; Rome and the western empire fell to invading barbarian tribes around 476, but the eastern empire, based at Constantinople, survived for another thousand years. Christianity also became divided during this time. The bishop of Rome (also known as the pope) claimed that all Christians should obey his decrees. The branch of the religion based on papal teachings became known as Roman Catholicism. Christian leaders in the eastern empire did not accept that the popes were the final authority on doctrine; instead, eastern bishops preferred to work in ecumenical councils where they could make their own decisions about doctrine. Because of the differences between the eastern Orthodox and Roman Catholic branches of Christianity, in 1054 a permanent schism occurred.

Today, the Eastern Orthodox Church is made up of many independent national churches, including Russian, Ukranian, and Greek. These churches share the same doctrine (based on ecumenical councils held between 325 and 787), and have similar liturgies and hierarchies of church leaders.

Most Russians respect the Orthodox Church as an important symbol of their cultural heritage. However, only a small minority are regular churchgoers. The casual attitude toward religion held by both Christians and Muslims may have helped spare Kazakhstan from the social unrest and violence occurring in nearby nations.

Lifestyles

From the 1920s through the 1980s, most Kazakhstanis lived in rural farming communities. Their pastoral lifestyles revolved around crops and

Ascension Cathedral is a Russian Orthodox house of worship located in a park in Almaty. Today there are almost as many Orthodox Christians in Kazakhstan as there are Muslims, but the number of Christians is falling as ethnic Russians leave the country.

livestock. Even today, some people still live on collective farms that were established early in the Soviet era. City life was principally for Russians who worked in business and industry.

Since independence, Kazakhstan's cities have grown rapidly. People from surrounding rural areas are moving to the city with hope of finding employment in the new economy. Some officials estimate that more than 2 million people, or 12 percent of the population, migrated from rural to urban areas during the 1990s alone. Only one in five Kazakhstani laborers still works in agriculture.

The sudden urban growth has led to overcrowding, public health problems, and high unemployment. Newcomers typically cannot find jobs or permanent housing, and so are unable to contribute to the city's tax base and do not appear in government census figures. In this troubled environment, city officials are hard-pressed to provide basic services such as law enforcement, education, and health care.

As difficult as city life may be, it is still considered preferable to life in the countryside, where poverty is rampant. Overall, 26 percent of Kazakhstanis live below the poverty line. Yet in some rural regions, the poverty rate has climbed as high as 55 percent. In a desperate attempt to generate income, a number of farmers have begun raising crops like the opium poppy, which is used to produce the illicit drug heroin.

Some people in the northern steppes still practice the nomadic lifestyle of their ancestors. Known as *shabans*, or shepherds, they roam the grazing lands with their livestock and live in tent-like dwellings called yurts.

Kazakh weddings and other celebrations feature unique food and drink, including fermented mare's milk and camel's milk. Traditional Kazakh cuisine is most popular in rural areas. The national dish is a type of potpie known as *besbarmak*. In addition to beef, it can be made with the meat of sheep or horses. *Qazy* is sausage made from horsemeat. Flatbread and tea are served with most meals. Dessert may include small doughnut balls called *baursaki* or a dish made from apples. Kazakh apples are prized throughout Central Asia. City dwellers typically enjoy a combination of Kazakh and Russian cuisine.

Western-style clothing has become the norm in Kazakhstan. Traditional clothing is sometimes worn at festivals and celebrations. For men, this includes a felt hat with baggy wool shirt and pants. Women wear long velvet dresses decorated with jewelry plus a fur hat with feathers. Kazakhstanis often add traditional pieces of clothing to their Western outfits, such as a felt hat with a business suit.

Life expectancy in Kazakhstan is short by Western standards. On average, Kazakhstanis live only to about age 66. The country's multitude of

Some people in Kazakhstan continue to live in the same way as their nomadic ancestors, traveling the lands with their livestock and living in traditional dwellings called yurts.

environmental problems is largely to blame, but poor health care is also a factor. Hospitals and clinics are ill equipped and understaffed. Patients must often be sent to Russia for treatment. Remote areas have experienced outbreaks of tuberculosis and other diseases. Drug abuse and HIV/AIDS infections are increasing among the nation's young people. Kazakhstan's government has only recently started taking steps to address these problems.

Arts and Entertainment

Kazakh art is influenced by indigenous culture and concepts from Russia and the Middle East. In nomadic times, art was limited to items that were both functional and mobile. Embroidered clothing and wool carpets were common forms of expression. Islam forbids the depiction of living things in art, so Kazakh weavers decorated fabrics with elaborate and colorful patterns. During the Soviet era, art served as propaganda for the communist program and included sculptures and paintings of Soviet historical figures.

Music has always been an important part of Kazakh culture. Traveling musicians known as *aqyns* still wander the countryside today. They sing folk tunes and recite ancient legends and poems. Contests between *aqyns* draw large crowds. Traditional Kazakh instruments include the two-stringed *dombyra*, which resembles a lute, and the three-stringed *kobiz*, which resembles a violin. Russian influence brought European opera and symphony to Kazakhstan's larger cities.

Written Kazakh literature was virtually nonexistent until the 19th century. Before then, storytelling was the pastime of nomads, who could not read. The father of Kazakh literature was Abay Kunanbayev, who lived from 1845 to 1904. He wrote poems and translated foreign literature into the Kazakh language. Kunanbayev's work inspired a new generation of Kazakh authors in the early 1900s, although many were imprisoned or executed during Joseph Stalin's purges. Playwright and novelist Mukhtar Auezov, who died in 1961, is considered Kazakhstan's most important modern literary figure.

A lasting benefit of Soviet rule is a solid educational system. Kazakhstan boasts a literacy rate that is over 98 percent, which compares

Kazakhstanis still play a traditional word game called *aitys*, in which two people exchange quips, boasts, and puns. The person who first runs out of clever replies is the loser.

A performance featuring Kazakh musicians and dancers.

favorably to most modernized nations, and its citizens are schooled in science and the arts. The country has roughly 1,200 newspapers and 500 magazines, plus dozens of radio and television stations. The government either owns or has strong ties to the largest media outlets, however, and exercises increasing control over the privately owned ones.

It is often difficult for Kazakhstanis to stay in touch with distant friends and relatives. Only about 20 percent of households have a telephone. Less than 3 percent of the population has access to the Internet. The postal service is extremely slow and unreliable. The government has given priority to modernizing the nation's communication systems. However, in a country as large as Kazakhstan, such improvements come slowly.

Kazakhstanis devote much leisure time to visiting nearby family members, going on picnics, and attending sporting events, as well as attending art exhibits and the theater and going to the movies. Soccer and horse racing are among the most popular spectator sports. A traditional game called *kokpar,* which involves two teams on horseback dragging around a goat carcass, is also popular.

Ice hockey became prevalent under the Soviets. Kazakhstan sends men's and women's teams to play in most international hockey tournaments, including the Olympics. As in other former Soviet republics, professional ice hockey offers young athletes an opportunity to escape poverty. A number of Kazakhstani hockey players have gone on to successful careers in North America, where the pay is considerably higher. One such player is Evgeni Nabokov, who became a starting goaltender in the National Hockey League during the 2000–01 season. Nabokov is from the mining town of Kamenogorsk in eastern Kazakhstan. He recorded 32 victories with the San Jose Sharks that season and was named the league's top rookie.

Ornate tilework decorates this large mosque in Zharkent. The small city in eastern Kazakhstan is located near the border with China.

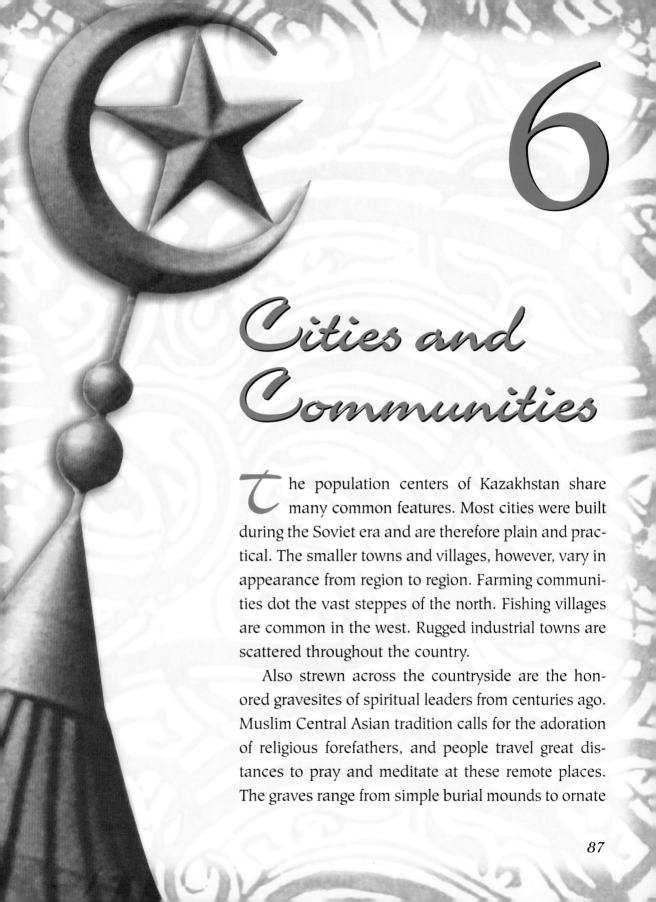

6

Cities and Communities

The population centers of Kazakhstan share many common features. Most cities were built during the Soviet era and are therefore plain and practical. The smaller towns and villages, however, vary in appearance from region to region. Farming communities dot the vast steppes of the north. Fishing villages are common in the west. Rugged industrial towns are scattered throughout the country.

Also strewn across the countryside are the honored gravesites of spiritual leaders from centuries ago. Muslim Central Asian tradition calls for the adoration of religious forefathers, and people travel great distances to pray and meditate at these remote places. The graves range from simple burial mounds to ornate stone mausoleums. Many have been restored to their original splendor since the breakup of the Soviet Union.

Cities in Kazakhstan are generally small. In terms of population, only Almaty comes close to North American standards. With a population of about 1.2 million, Almaty is nearly as large as Dallas. However, no other Kazakh city approaches this size. Kazakhstan's 1999 census found that Almaty is the only city to contain more than half a million people. A total of only 26 cities had more than 50,000 residents. This number will certainly increase as Kazakhstanis continue to migrate from rural to metropolitan areas.

Since independence, many cities and streets have been renamed. The original Russian names, which were given by Soviet officials, have been changed to Kazakh names. Only in the north, where a large Russian population still exists, have the original names been retained.

Almaty

Far to the southeast, near the border with Kyrgyzstan, lies Almaty. Aside from being Kazakhstan's largest city, it is also largely regarded as one of the most important cities in Central Asia.

Almaty was founded first as a Russian fort in 1854. The outpost's occupants soon realized that the area was prone to earthquakes. In 1887, a violent tremor nearly destroyed the fort and the settlement that had grown around it. The settlers found that the local climate was ideal for growing apples, and orchards appeared everywhere. Another quake hit in 1911, and once again the settlers rebuilt their homes. The new town was called Alma-Ata, which means "Father of Apples" in Kazakh.

By 1930, Alma-Ata had a population of about 50,000. It was designated the capital of the Kazakh S.S.R., and connected to the rest of the Soviet Union by rail. The city grew rapidly during World War II, as industry and workers arrived from war-torn western Russia. Following the war, Alma-Ata

Residents of Almaty walk through a courtyard in Abai Square. Almaty is Kazakhstan's largest city, with a population of about 1.2 million people.

continued to grow. In addition to being the seat of government, it became Kazakhstan's cultural heart. The city is home to most of the country's museums and theaters.

For decades, the city lived quietly under Soviet rule until violence struck in 1986. Moscow selected an ethnic Russian politician to lead Kazakhstan's government, and residents took to the streets in protest. When word spread of the Alma-Ata uprising, riots broke out in other cities as well. Soviet police responded harshly and an unknown number of demonstrators were killed. Afterward, the government tried to blame the riots on drunken college students, but most people knew the truth. Five years later, Kazakhstan declared its independence from the Soviet Union on the anniversary of the Alma-Ata uprising. The city was renamed Almaty.

President Nazarbayev's decision to relocate the government to Astana has had little impact on Almaty. Although no longer the nation's capital, Almaty continues to grow and remains important as a financial hub. Kazakhstan's banking system is still based in the city, and most of the country's international transactions occur there. Russians continue to be the dominant ethnic group in Almaty as they did before, but now business professionals from all over the world work beside them.

Almaty has no skyscrapers. Since the city is frequently shaken by tremors, hardly any buildings are more than a few stories high. Almaty has a multitude of parks and tree-lined streets. It has been said that the combination of towering trees and squat buildings gives Almaty the appearance

This war memorial in Almaty commemorates the men from Kazakhstan who served with the Soviet army during World War II.

of a city in a forest. In the background, the snowcapped peaks of the Zailiysky Alatau mountain range stretch into the sky.

Astana

As the new capital, Astana is one of Kazakhstan's fastest growing cities. During the 1990s its population increased by 13 percent. Yet with just 313,000 residents, Astana lags far behind Almaty and is only the fifth-largest city in Kazakhstan.

Like Almaty, Astana began as a Russian military outpost in the mid-19th century. Located in the center of the fertile Kazakh steppes, the town became known for its surplus of dairy products and fresh bread. It originally took the name Aqmola, which in Kazakh means "white burial mound." The town's reputation as an agricultural paradise earned it respect in the 1960s. The Soviet plan to boost grain and cotton production, known as the Virgin Lands program, needed a headquarters. Aqmola was chosen for that purpose and was renamed Tselinograd, Russian for "virgin lands city." Tens of thousands of Russian administrators and engineers poured into the city as the project got underway.

As the Virgins Lands campaign declined, the city slowly faded into obscurity. Following independence in 1991, the original Kazakh name of Aqmola was restored. However, Russians remained the dominant ethnic group in the city. Only about one in five residents was Kazakh. At the time, nobody imagined that Aqmola would soon become the nation's capital.

President Nazarbayev first announced his intentions to transfer the capital in 1994. Kazakhstanis were puzzled by the decision. Aqmola was a small, run-down city with a reputation for severe winters. Nazarbayev said he wanted to move the government away from the earthquakes of Almaty, but most people suspected he also had political motives. Aqmola's location near the center of the country would allow the government to keep a closer eye on the Russian population of the north. Aqmola was renamed Astana and construction began.

Nazarbayev assured the taxpayers of Kazakhstan that they would not have to pay for the construction costs. Instead, he would solicit donations from foreign corporations and elsewhere. Western oil companies in particular were pressured to make generous contributions, which they did. Ultimately, hundreds of millions of dollars were raised for construction purposes, but rumors swirled that much of the money was instead being diverted into private bank accounts. Several buildings for which some of the donations were earmarked have yet to be built.

The government was officially transferred to Astana in late 1997. Although years have passed since the move, Almaty remains the center of

A public square in Astana, which became the capital of Kazakhstan in 1997. It is one of the country's fastest-growing cities.

activity in Kazakhstan. Many legislators and other officials refuse to live full-time in the new capital. Instead, they constantly shuttle back and forth between Astana and Almaty. A few museums and attractions have opened in Astana, but most remain in Almaty. The government's presence has, however, altered the ethnic makeup of the city. Ethnic Kazakhs now account for more than 40 percent of the population.

Northern Kazakhstan

The country's northern regions are the traditional lands of Kazakh nomads. For centuries, clans wandered the steppes and raised their herds on the rich grasses. In the 1800s, Russian settlements interrupted the nomadic Kazakh lifestyle, and the new Soviet system in the 1920s put an end to it. Yet the ancient grazing lands remained an important symbol of Kazakh culture. During the breakup of the Soviet Union, many Kazakhs feared that the Russian population of the north would attempt to make the steppes part of Russia.

Those fears have since abated. Kazakhs and Russians alike are now focused on making a living in agriculture and industry. Much of Kazakhstan's mineral wealth is concentrated in the north, and many cities exist to support nearby mines and foundries. Qaraghandy is one such city.

In the 1930s, Qaraghandy, also known as Karaganda, was little more than a collection of Soviet prison camps. The Soviet Union, which was undergoing an industrial revolution at the time, needed fuel for its factories. The Qaraghandy area was rich in coal, and some of Joseph Stalin's countless political prisoners were sent to mine it. Labor camps were common across the Soviet Union until the mid-1950s. An uprising took place at the Kengir prison camp near Qaraghandy in 1954. The rebellion was violently crushed with troops and tanks, and hundreds of prisoners were killed. Shortly afterward, the labor camp system was abandoned.

Today, Qaraghandy is the second-largest city in Kazakhstan with a population of 438,000. Coal mining continues to play a major role in the local economy, but steel has become the dominant industry. The Qaraghandy Metallurgical Combine, or Karmet, is among the largest steel mills in the world. For decades the city was plagued by severe industrial pollution. While the environmental problems have been addressed in recent years, there is a new health threat: Qaraghandy has the highest percentage of HIV/AIDS cases in the country.

Kazakhstan's northernmost city, Petropavlovsk, is less than 40 miles (60 km) from the Russian border. With 203,000 residents, mostly ethnic Russians, it is the 11th-largest city in Kazakhstan. During Soviet times, Petropavlovsk was heavily guarded because its factories produced top-secret military equipment. Currently, the city serves as a staging area for trade goods traveling to and from Russia.

Southern Kazakhstan

Far to the south, near the border with Uzbekistan, lies the ancient city of Shymkent. During the 12th century, Shymkent was a resting place for caravans traveling along the Silk Road. Visitors from distant lands brought wealth and new ideas to the thriving metropolis, making Shymkent a cultural center for Kazakhstan. The city's key location also placed it in the path of danger, and throughout its history Shymkent has withstood countless battles and invasions.

During the 1930s, Shymkent was transformed into a rail junction and industrial center. Newly built factories produced textiles, pharmaceuticals, and refined metals. During World War II, Soviet pilots trained for combat at a nearby airbase. Afterward, the city continued to flourish and by the 1980s its population approached 500,000.

Many ethnic Russians left Shymkent after independence, and as a result the population currently stands at about 358,000. Still, it is the third-largest city in Kazakhstan. Food processing has replaced some of the older industries, and foodstuffs produced in Shymkent are transported throughout Central Asia.

Not far from Shymkent is the country's fourth-largest city, Taraz. Shymkent and Taraz share a similar history as Silk Road stops, but Taraz's history dates back as far as the fifth century. Taraz was part of an ancient Islamic kingdom before Genghis Khan destroyed the city in the 13th century. It was rebuilt several hundred years later, only to be conquered by the Russians.

Unlike Shymkent, Taraz has seen its population grow since independence. Ethnic Kazakhs are moving into the city faster than ethnic Russians are moving out. Taraz has 326,000 residents, most of whom are Kazakh. The city is best known for its vodka, but it also produces food, fertilizer, and textiles.

Because southern Kazakhstan has the highest percentage of ethnic Kazakhs, it is more Muslim than other parts of the country. The small city of Turkistan, about 100 miles (160 kilometers) northwest of Shymkent, is home to the most important Islamic site in all of Kazakhstan. During the 12th century, a highly respected Muslim cleric named Ahmad Yasawi lived in Turkistan. After his death, an elaborate shrine was built to honor this holy man. The shrine has an enormous vaulted ceiling that is the largest intact dome in Central Asia. In the 1950s, the monument was closed down

> **The small town of Zharkent in eastern Kazakhstan has a unique mosque that was built in the 19th century. In addition to featuring traditional Islamic design, the wooden mosque also contains architectural styles from both China and Russia. It is a special reminder of Kazakhstan's multicultural history.**

by Soviet officials and surrounded with barbed wire. It reopened in the 1980s and has since been restored. For Kazakh Muslims, a pilgrimage to Turkistan is almost as important as a pilgrimage to Mecca.

Near the center of Kazakhstan is a different type of landmark: a space-operations center known as the Baykonur Cosmodrome. In 1961, Soviet cosmonaut Yuri Gagarin climbed aboard his spacecraft on a Baykonur launchpad and became the first human to hurtle into space. Every manned Russian spaceflight has originated in Baykonur, which explains why Russia was eager to negotiate a lease for the facility following Kazakhstan's independence. Even today, the cosmodrome and the towns that support it are tightly controlled by the Russian military. While Baykonur is officially listed as a Kazakh oblast, surrounding it is an area of 6,000 square miles (16,000 sq km) that is effectively Russian-held territory. The number of people living in this area is unknown, and Kazakhstanis have very little contact with them.

Eastern Kazakhstan

The towns and cities of eastern Kazakhstan have steadily shrunk over the past two decades. People continue to flee the lingering effects of Soviet nuclear testing. Radioactive contamination has also reduced the average lifespan and birth rate in the region, contributing further to the population loss.

The city that was closest to the nuclear tests, Semey, has seen the most dramatic decreases. Semey's already dwindling population fell an additional 15 percent during the 1990s. About 270,000 residents still remain, making Semey the eighth-largest city in Kazakhstan. As Semey's population continues to decline, so does its economy and political power. In 1997, the city lost its status as capital of the eastern oblast.

Like so many other Kazakh cities, Semey started out as a Russian fortress. The fort was built to help ward off an invasion by Mongolian

A trolley passes a billboard advertising the electric and heat services of a multinational company in the city of Öskemen, in eastern Kazakhstan.

hordes in the 1700s. Fertile soil and the nearby Irtysh River aided agriculture, and the settlement grew into a major producer of cotton, meat, wool, and leather goods. The pastoral tradition continues in the region, though radioactive contamination of crops and livestock is a major concern.

Semey also has a rich intellectual tradition. Many of Kazakhstan's great literary figures, including Abay Kunanbayev and Mukhtar Auezov, came from Semey. In the 1920s, Semey was home to the ill-fated Kazakh independence movement, known as Alash Orda. The city has an acclaimed university that, despite the health risks, still attracts students from all over Asia.

Other major cities in eastern Kazakhstan include Öskemen and Pavlodar. Öskemen is the sixth-largest city with 311,000 residents, while

Pavlodar is the seventh-largest city with 300,000 residents. Both of these cities lie along the Irtysh River, and both are industrial towns. Mines surrounding Öskemen yield vast quantities of copper, lead, silver, and zinc. Pavlodar's factories once produced Soviet tanks, but now they manufacture tractors and other farm equipment.

Western Kazakhstan

The country's western regions have also seen drastic population loss due to environmental problems. The gradual destruction of the Aral Sea has been forcing people from their homes for over a quarter of a century. But unlike the east, western Kazakhstan was always very thinly populated, and the mass exodus of its residents has had an even more profound effect. Some communities have vanished entirely. Only petroleum and the Caspian Sea fishing industry provide incentive for Kazakhstanis to remain.

The surviving population centers of the west are situated along either the Caspian Sea coastline or near the Russian border. The largest of these, Aqtöbe, has 253,000 residents. Aqtöbe, formerly Aktyubinsk, is the only city in western Kazakhstan not to suffer a population decline during the 1990s. The mountains near Aqtöbe contain a rare mineral called chromite. Large deposits of chromite have been found in only a few places throughout the world. Aqtöbe has produced roughly one-fourth of the world's supply of the mineral. Additionally, major railways and oil pipelines pass through Aqtöbe, making it a key city in Kazakhstan's economy.

The Ural River flows from Russia through western Kazakhstan before emptying into the Caspian Sea. A port city called Atyraü straddles the Ural just before it reaches the Caspian. Though a small city, Atyraü is of major significance—it is at the heart of Kazakhstan's growing petroleum industry. Atyraü has been producing oil from surrounding fields for nearly a century. Yet many Western oil companies believe it is only beginning to reach its true potential.

Atyraü was founded in the 1640s as a Russian trading post and military base. From that point until 1993 the town was known as Guryev, which was the name of the Russian trader who founded it. Fishing was the primary industry, and the town became a leading supplier of caviar. In 1911, an oil refinery was built and petroleum took on increasing importance to the city throughout the 20th century. The bulk of Atyraü's oil comes from beneath the desert. However, once the Caspian's enormous deposits are tapped, Atyraü's petroleum output is expected to soar.

Flooding is a problem for Atyraü. The city receives excessive rainfall, and residents must often slog through ankle-deep mud. Additionally, each year the rising Caspian draws closer, prompting fears that someday the entire city will be underwater.

ҚСАТЫМЫЗ - ҚАЗАҚСТАННЫҢ ТЕРРИТО
ТАСТЫҒЫ МЕН ДЕРБЕСТІГІН ҚОРҒАУ"
Н.Ә. НАЗ

U.S. Secretary of Defense Donald Rumsfeld (right) and Kazakhstan's Minister of Defense General Muktar Altynbayev conduct a joint press conference, February 2004. After the September 11, 2001, terrorist attacks on the World Trade Center and the Pentagon, Kazakhstan offered to help the United States in its war against radical Islamist groups like al-Qaeda.

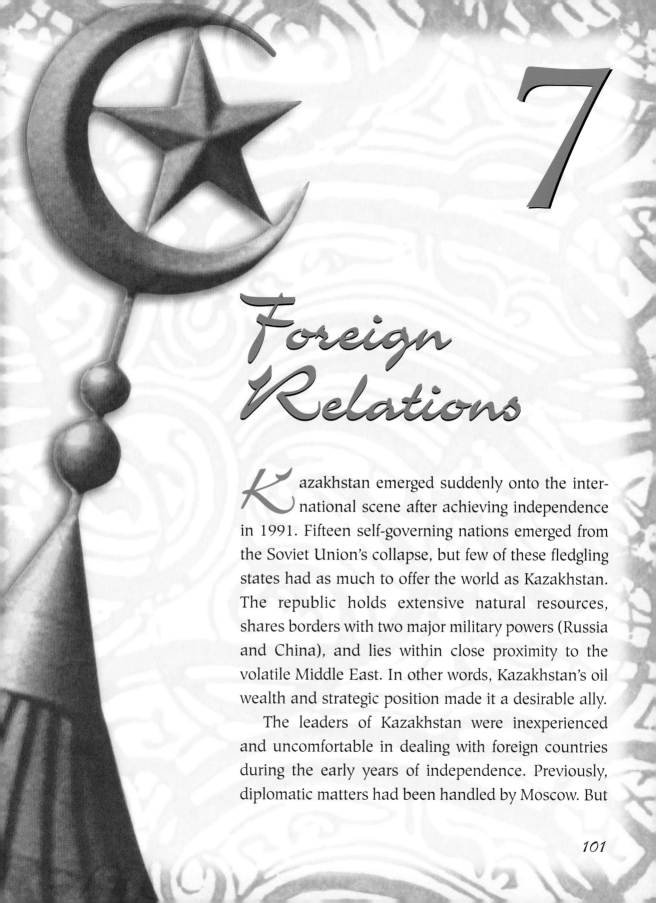

7

Foreign Relations

Kazakhstan emerged suddenly onto the international scene after achieving independence
in 1991. Fifteen self-governing nations emerged from
the Soviet Union's collapse, but few of these fledgling
states had as much to offer the world as Kazakhstan.
The republic holds extensive natural resources,
shares borders with two major military powers (Russia
and China), and lies within close proximity to the
volatile Middle East. In other words, Kazakhstan's oil
wealth and strategic position made it a desirable ally.

The leaders of Kazakhstan were inexperienced
and uncomfortable in dealing with foreign countries
during the early years of independence. Previously,
diplomatic matters had been handled by Moscow. But

as time passed and its ambassadors gained experience, Kazakhstan's government grew more confident. Today, Kazakhstan relishes its place in the global community and welcomes international contact.

Healthy relationships with the other Central Asian states will always be important to Kazakhstan. For religious reasons, the country also hopes to maintain a good rapport with the Muslim countries of the Middle East. Yet the Nazarbayev regime also has not hesitated to work with the West. Since 1991, the government has forged strong ties with the United States and other Western nations. Despite its many commitments, however, Kazakhstan still makes Russia its major priority in foreign policy.

Relations with Russia

Kazakhstan found itself in an unusual situation at the beginning of 1992. The republic had been granted an independence it did not particularly want. Soviet troops occupied military bases scattered across the country, but once they went home Kazakhstan would be left virtually defenseless. Economically, the new nation was still very much dependent on Russia. It is therefore not surprising that President Nazarbayev immediately tried to create a close alliance between Kazakhstan and Russia.

Moscow, on the other hand, had little interest in an alliance with Kazakhstan. Like most of the other former Soviet republics, Russia was eager to modernize its economy. The Russians felt that a close relationship with the needy Kazakhstanis would only slow their progress. Whenever Nazarbayev proposed a treaty, Russia's leaders made unreasonable demands that they knew Nazarbayev could not accept. In late 1993, Russia declared that if Kazakhstan wished to continue using Russian currency, it would have to turn its gold reserves over to Moscow. At this point, Nazarbayev finally began charting an independent course for his country.

Even after Kazakhstan established its own currency and a capable military, the Nazarbayev government remained sensitive to Russian interests.

The northern neighbor was easily Kazakhstan's largest trading partner, and the only buyer of many Kazakh exports. Furthermore, Kazakhstan's defense force was no match for the powerful Russian military. Nazarbayev was careful not to take any steps that might anger either Moscow or his country's ethnic Russian citizens.

As Kazakhstan developed relationships with other countries during the mid-1990s, the Nazarbayev regime became less concerned about the threat from Russia. The two nations squabbled over Kazakhstan's growing oil revenues. Russia claimed that it deserved a share of the profits because Kazakhstan's oil industry had been built by the Soviet Union. Kazakhstan strongly refuted this argument. Ultimately, a compromise was reached in which Kazakhstan paid Russia royalties to transport Kazakh oil through Russian pipelines.

Russian and Kazakhstani officials sign a friendship treaty between the two countries, March 1992. In recent years the two neighbors have worked together on economic development projects.

The two countries also reached an agreement on the Baykonur Cosmodrome, located in central Kazakhstan. The space center is Russia's only facility for launching manned space flights. In 1994, Russia began paying Kazakhstan $115 million per year to use the center. In early 2004, the contract was extended through 2050. Baykonur became extremely important in February 2003, when the space shuttle *Columbia* disaster grounded the U.S. space fleet. A series of launches from Baykonur carried replacement crews to the international space station orbiting the Earth.

Today, Kazakhstan and Russia understand that they need one another in order to achieve economic prosperity. As a landlocked nation, Kazakhstan must send its exports across Russian soil in order to reach vital sea routes. For its part, Russia hopes to benefit from Kazakhstan's growing economy. Russians no longer view Kazakhstan as a potential burden, but rather as a potential partner. In 2000, both countries entered into the Eurasian Economic Community along with three other former Soviet republics—Belarus, Kyrgyzstan, and Tajikistan. The alliance hopes to eventually develop a powerful trade zone.

In 2002, Russia and Kazakhstan agreed to work together on developing the oilfields beneath the Caspian Sea. In 2003, trade revenue between the two reached a record $5 billion. Also at that time, a joint cultural program designated 2003 as the "Year of Kazakhstan in Russia" and 2004 as the "Year of Russia in Kazakhstan." Both nations appear optimistic about their future together.

Relations with China and Uzbekistan

Kazakhstan's friendship with China is less certain. The long, mountainous border with China had never been clearly defined, and during the 1990s the two countries bickered over the boundary's precise location. Although this dispute has been largely resolved, the border remains a source of friction between the Chinese and Kazakh governments. Neither country can adequately patrol the remote area. As a result, it has become a gateway for illegal immigration, drug smuggling, and other illicit activities.

The Nazarbayev regime now considers China a greater threat than Russia. The Chinese army is enormous—the number of Chinese troops stationed within striking distance of Kazakhstan is estimated to be three times the size of Kazakhstan's defense force. China has never shown any aggression toward Kazakhstan, however. Both are members of a regional security alliance called the Shanghai Cooperation Organization, and in December 2002 leaders of the two countries signed a treaty of friendship and cooperation. Nevertheless, China poses a potential danger that cannot be overlooked.

Lucrative trade deals have broadened the relationship between China and Kazakhstan. The robust Chinese economy devours Kazakh raw materials, especially petroleum and steel. In 1997, Kazakhstan sold China the

A view of the Shanghai Cooperation Organization (SCO) summit in Uzbekistan, June 2004, during which presidents of the member nations met to discuss terrorism and increased economic and military cooperation along their common borders. The organization, which was formally established in 2001, grew out of efforts in the 1990s to strengthen confidence-building measures in the border regions and fight regional terrorism, religious extremism, and separatism.

drilling rights to an oilfield that was originally earmarked for Western companies. Plans to build an oil pipeline into western China have frequently been discussed.

Kazakhstan's southeastern neighbor, Uzbekistan, poses a different type of security risk. The Kazakh and Uzbek people share a common heritage; centuries ago they both sprang from the same horde. But while the Kazakhs chose to remain nomadic, the Uzbeks settled down to farm. Sedentary lifestyles foster different religious practice than migratory ways of living. As a result, the practice of Islam is more traditional in Uzbekistan than it is in Kazakhstan.

In 1998, an extremist group known as the Islamic Movement of Uzbekistan (IMU) formed. The ultimate goal of the IMU is to transform Central Asia into an Islamic state. Between 1999 and 2001, the IMU launched a series of attacks throughout the region. Although Kazakhstan was spared from the incursions, some attacks took place within miles of the Kazakhstan border. Further, IMU agents began recruiting new members in Kazakhstan's poverty-stricken south.

The IMU was affiliated with the extremist group known as the Taliban, which had seized control of Afghanistan in 1996 and imposed strict Islamic law within the areas of the country it controlled. The Taliban also harbored Osama bin Laden and his terrorist organization, al-Qaeda. When U.S. forces invaded Afghanistan in response to the terrorist attacks of September 11, 2001, the IMU rushed to the aid of the Taliban and al-Qaeda. IMU fighters suffered heavy losses in the combat that followed.

A smaller, reorganized version of the IMU still operates in Central Asia. Other extremist groups have joined its cause. In early 2004, the Uzbek cities of Tashkent and Bukhara were rocked by terror bombings that killed dozens of people. Many analysts believe that Uzbekistan's president, Islam Karimov, encourages extremism because of his authoritarian style of government. After the terror bombings in Tashkent and Bukhara,

Two women walk near a crossing post at the border between Uzbekistan and Kazakhstan. The post uses sensitive radiation detectors in an effort to control smuggling of nuclear materials from former Soviet states. The U.S. donated the detectors as part of a program to train Central Asian customs officials and provide state-of-the-art detection equipment. Experts say that lax controls on nuclear material created during the Soviet era makes Central Asia attractive to terrorists trying to create a "dirty bomb" laced with radioactive materials.

Karimov's secret police arrested and tortured hundreds of citizens who were believed to oppose the government.

The volatile events in Uzbekistan make the government of Kazakhstan uneasy. A large-scale uprising against the Karimov regime could easily spill over into southern Kazakhstan, which has a sizable ethnic Uzbek population. Terrorists already cross the border into southern Kazakhstan with relative ease.

Relations with Other Muslim Nations

Extremist groups also plague Turkmenistan, Tajikistan, and Kyrgyzstan. Turkmenistan is a desert nation that has been subjected to authoritarian rule since it gained independence from the Soviet Union. Tajikistan and Kyrgyzstan are rugged, mountainous regions that contain plenty of hiding places for terrorist training camps. Both Tajikistan and Kyrgyzstan have experimented with democracy, but those efforts have been hindered by severe poverty and social unrest. Further instability in any of the Central Asian states could have perilous consequences for Kazakhstan.

The government of Kazakhstan takes a neutral approach toward the Islamic nations that constitute the Middle East. Meanwhile, Muslim fundamentalists in those nations generally regard Kazakhstanis as believers who lost their way during the Soviet era. Since 1991, several Middle Eastern organizations have attempted to educate Kazakhstanis in the ways of traditional Islam. Such attempts have not been welcomed by the secular Nazarbayev regime.

Religious differences aside, Kazakhstan and the countries of the Middle East have much to gain by working together. The world's largest oil **cartel**, the Organization of Petroleum Exporting Countries (OPEC), recognizes the potential of a partnership. In 2001, a Saudi official suggested that Kazakhstan become an OPEC member. However, Nazarbayev expressed little interest in the idea, and in late 2003 proposed the creation of a separate cartel consisting of Caspian Sea oil producers, a group that also includes Azerbaijan, Turkmenistan, and Uzbekistan. His suggestion was met with only lukewarm support from the other Caspian nations, however.

A pipeline through Iran to the Persian Gulf would be an ideal outlet for Kazakhstan's Caspian Sea oil. However, most international observers consider an Iranian pipeline unlikely in the near future. As Kazakhstan's largest foreign investor, the United States would need to approve the project. Given the unfriendly nature of U.S.-Iran relations, the prospects for such an approval are highly doubtful.

Relations with the West

The United States was the first country to officially recognize Kazakhstan as an independent nation in December 1991. An American embassy opened in Almaty less than one month later. The U.S. government had many reasons to quickly establish a friendship with Kazakhstan. Aside from its interest in Kazakh oil, the United States wanted to encourage the new nation to embrace democracy. Additionally, the Soviet military had left behind more than 1,300 nuclear warheads in Kazakhstan. U.S. officials were concerned that those weapons could fall into the hands of terrorists or rogue nations.

Kazakh leaders welcomed a relationship with the United States, because they hoped it would help deter any possible aggression by the Russian military. Further, Nazarbayev wanted to rid his country of the Soviet nuclear weapons and he knew the United States would gladly help. In 1994, Kazakhstan began dismantling its nuclear arsenal with assistance from American engineers. The U.S. government spent $188 million to help Kazakhstan become a nuclear-free state.

The American-Kazakh relationship grew even stronger after the terrorist attacks of September 11, 2001. Kazakhstan declared itself an ally in the U.S.-led war on terror. President Nazarbayev offered the use of Kazakh

U.S. military aid to Kazakhstan has included helicopters and cargo planes, as well as coast guard boats for patrolling the Caspian Sea.

General Altynbayev and Secretary Rumsfeld receive a briefing during the U.S. Secretary of Defense's 2004 visit to Astana.

airspace to U.S. warplanes that were hunting for terrorists in Afghanistan. Following the invasion of Iraq in 2003, Nazarbayev sent a small Kazakh peacekeeping unit that disarmed more than 100,000 landmines across war-torn Iraq. In early 2004, Defense Secretary Donald Rumsfeld traveled to Kazakhstan and expressed gratitude for the assistance it gave the United States.

Cooperation between the two countries goes well beyond national security issues. The U.S. government strongly supported Kazakhstan's conversion to a market economy. During the 1990s, American economic advisors provided guidance on issues such as banking reform, pension management, and monetary policy. More recently, the United States and Kazakhstan have entered into a number of partnerships regarding energy production and business development.

However, the United States remains concerned about the government of Kazakhstan's unwillingness to adopt democratic reforms. In 2003, the

U.S. government provided $92 million in aid to Kazakhstan. Nearly $14 million was intended to advance human rights, freedom of speech, and government accountability. The remainder funded a variety of social, economic, and military programs. U.S. officials have taken a careful approach toward the Nazarbayev regime. They hope to persuade the Kazakh president to accept democracy without alienating him at the same time.

Kazakhstan has close ties with other Western nations as well. Germany, Italy, and France are important trading partners. British and Canadian companies have invested heavily in Kazakhstan's industry. Furthermore, Kazakhstan participates in military exercises with the North Atlantic Treaty Organization (NATO), a defense alliance of countries in Europe and North America. In the 1990s, NATO invited the former Soviet republics to take part in training operations and information sharing. Kazakhstan eagerly accepted the invitation.

The government of Kazakhstan must manage its foreign affairs carefully. Russia, China, the Middle East, and the West all have competing interests. Some of Kazakhstan's partners, such as Russia and China, harbor deep suspicions toward one another. Several nations in the Middle East are openly hostile toward the West. Accordingly, Kazakhstan must maintain good relations with each partner yet at the same time not antagonize the others.

The Future

International observers are impressed by the diplomatic skills of President Nazarbayev and his ambassadors. It has often been reported that Nazarbayev never traveled abroad prior to 1990. Yet within a decade, he managed to learn the intricacies of foreign diplomacy and build a generally favorable position for Kazakhstan. Governments from around the world now watch and wonder what path Kazakhstan will take next.

To some extent, President Nazarbayev has already outlined his plans for the future. In 1998, he produced a report entitled *Kazakhstan 2030*.

Providing short-term and long-term objectives, the document describes Nazarbayev's vision of the country's progress during the next three decades. Subjects covered in the report include national security, economic growth, and social welfare. In essence, *Kazakhstan 2030* was intended to be the country's roadmap to prosperity.

Unfortunately, *Kazakhstan 2030* is a vague document filled with metaphors and flowery language. Within its pages, President Nazarbayev describes many lofty goals for Kazakhstan, but he offers few details on how they will be attained. The report frequently skims over the government's responsibilities and instead advises common citizens on steps they must take to improve the nation. For example, Kazakhstanis are encouraged to adopt healthier lifestyles, be more tolerant of one another, and take pride in their country.

The report's chapter on national security offers some insight on the Nazarbayev regime's current strategy. The Kazakh president asserts that maintaining friendships with both Russia and China is the government's top priority. The next priority is good relations with the other Central Asian states and the Middle East. Nazarbayev then acknowledges the United States and other Western nations as important allies. Finally, he states that Kazakhstan should not rely entirely on protection from other nations, and that a strong defense force is the best deterrent against armed conflict. The Kazakh government's annual increases in military spending suggest that it still subscribes to this belief.

Kazakhstan 2030 makes little reference to implementing democratic reforms. It seems clear that the Nazarbayev regime no longer considers democracy a necessity for Kazakhstan. Instead, government officials have become bolder in their insistence that Kazakhstanis are not prepared to live in a democracy. They argue that sweeping changes would weaken the country's social fabric and make it vulnerable to extremism. The government of Kazakhstan seems to have recognized that it is unlikely any country will try to force Kazakhstan to become more democratic. Although the United States and other Western nations would like to see Kazakhstan become a more free and open society, these foreign states will not press too hard for reforms for fear of disrupting their access to Kazakhstan's petroleum.

Nazarbayev appears to have adopted the strategy of taking token steps toward democracy in order to appease his Western allies. In early 2004, he approved modest changes to the electoral process. Later that spring, he vetoed legislation that would have expanded the government's already considerable control over the media.

Simultaneously, the government of Kazakhstan has stepped up its efforts to shape world opinion of the country. Lobbyists in Washington, D.C., and other Western capitals have been hired to enhance Kazakhstan's image and divert attention away from negative news reports. Kazakhstan's embassies around the world maintain stylish web sites that present the country in a positive light and tout the latest democratic, economic, and social reforms.

International watchdog agencies describe an environment in Kazakhstan that is much different from the one portrayed by lobbyists and public relations firms. Since 1999, the Organization for Security and Cooperation in Europe (OSCE) has found that elections in Kazakhstan fall far short of international standards. OSCE observers report that opposition candidates are denied access to the media; local government officials interfere with the electoral process; and some vote-counting methods are highly questionable. The Nazarbayev government says it is currently working with OSCE to resolve these problems.

In April 2004, the organization Human Rights Watch (HRW) released a study on the lack of political freedom in Kazakhstan. HRW found that the government of Kazakhstan continues to file false criminal charges against its most vocal critics. The report cited the case of Sergei Duvanov, a journalist who frequently wrote about government corruption. In 2003, Duvanov was arrested on child molestation charges and sent to prison for three and a half years. Most political observers believe the charges were fabricated. HRW also found that the government actively discourages people from running for office. Potential opposition candidates are told to either withdraw or they will face legal trouble and unemployment.

Each year, the group Transparency International conducts a worldwide survey of government corruption. People from 133 countries are asked to rate the integrity of their public officials. Each country then receives a score between zero and ten based on the responses. A score of zero represents high corruption while a score of ten represents high integrity. In 2003, Kazakhstan received a score of just 2.4, finishing behind such notoriously corrupt nations as Argentina and the Philippines.

Allegations of government corruption in Kazakhstan reach as high up as the president. In 2003, U.S. prosecutors accused an American oil executive of making illegal payments of more than $78 million. When the charges were initially filed, the names of the bribe takers were kept secret. However, in early 2004, federal prosecutors revealed that the bribe recipients were Nazarbayev and a former prime minister, Akezhan Kazhegeldin. The government of Kazakhstan declined to comment on the allegations.

Despite all its shortcomings, the Nazarbayev administration is less repressive than some neighboring regimes. While the government of Kazakhstan may be guilty of neglecting its citizens, it cannot be accused of widespread torture or murder. It is also far more sensitive to religious and ethnic issues than other Central Asian governments. As a result, democratic nations around the world continue to hold out hope for Kazakhstan. If its government can learn to use its power responsibly, Kazakhstan may someday become a model of freedom and liberty for the entire region.

Kazakhstanis may need to wait for a new leader before seeing true democratic reform. Although President Nazarbayev seemed to show genuine

President Nazarbayev receives an electronic ballot device at a polling station before the September 2004 parliamentary election. The president's Otan party received a majority of the vote, but opposition leaders complained that the election was rigged. Use of the electronic system was controversial, for example, because it left no paper record. Although Nazarbayev had promised the election would be "free and fair," afterward international observers from the Organisation for Security and Cooperation in Europe (OSCE) reported it "fell short of OSCE commitments and other international standards for democratic elections." Although the OSCE noted some improvements—no media outlets were shut down or journalists imprisoned, for example—it said state and local government officials exercised "considerable pressure" on voters.

interest in implementing democracy during the early 1990s, as a product of the Soviet political system he eventually reverted to the leadership style that he knew best.

Many people believe that Nazarbayev's daughter, Dariga Nazarbayeva, is destined to become the next president of Kazakhstan. She is a powerful businesswoman and said to be politically adept. Although her rise to the presidency would most likely occur via less-than-democratic means, most

Dariga Nazarbayeva listens as her father speaks at a press conference in Almaty. The daughter of the president is the head of a separate political party, Asar ("All Together"), which holds the second-largest number of seats in the assembly. Her growing power has fueled speculations about a possible Nazarbayev family ruling dynasty in Kazakhstan.

Kazakhstanis probably would not complain. Since the time of the nomadic hordes, leaders have traditionally passed power on to their kin. Therefore, Kazakh society is likely to accept Dariga Nazarbayeva, or another hand-picked family member, as the next president. Perhaps that person will be more committed to change than the current president.

Economically, it is obvious that Kazakhstan will depend on its abundance of natural resources for some time to come. If the surging flow of oil revenue is used wisely in coming years, Kazakhstan should be able to clean up the environment, build a modern infrastructure, and improve its standard of living. The decision to set up the National Oil Fund is an important step toward ensuring that Kazakhstan will have a solid financial future after its oil reserves are finally exhausted or the world demand for petroleum declines.

The future of Islam in Kazakhstan is unclear. The secular government grudgingly tolerates Islam and other religions out of recognition that religious persecution only breeds further discontent. However, if Islamic extremist groups from Uzbekistan and elsewhere were to succeed in bringing terrorism to Kazakhstan, a government crackdown could ensue. Barring this scenario, Islam will likely remain what it has always been in Kazakhstan—a peaceful source of strength and comfort in people's lives.

Eighth century B.C.	The Scythians spread across Central Asia and into the region of present-day Kazakhstan.
First century B.C.	The Scythians leave Central Asia for India; nomadic tribes begin roaming the steppes.
A.D. **751**	Arab forces defeat Chinese forces at the Battle of Talas near southern Kazakhstan, opening the way for Islam into Central Asia.
1219	Genghis Khan conquers the region.
1227	Genghis Khan dies and his empire is split among his heirs; the Kazakh region is brought under control of the Golden Horde.
Late 1400s	The Kazakhs break away from the Golden Horde and create their own khanate.
Late 1500s	The Kazakh Khanate splits into the Great Horde, the Middle Horde, and the Little Horde.
1680–1720	A series of Mongol invasions devastates the Kazakh hordes during a period known as the Great Disaster.
Mid-1700s	Russia agrees to protect the Kazakh hordes in return for payments and loyalty to the czar; Russian settlers begin moving to the steppes.
1848	The czar abolishes the Kazakh hordes.
1916	Kazakhs rebel against Russian rule; some fight while others flee to China.
Early 1920's	Kazakhstan becomes an autonomous republic of the Soviet Union; Kazakhstan is gripped by a famine that kills over a million people.
1928	The Soviets force Kazakhs to move onto government-owned farms.
Early 1940s	Workers and industries from western Russia are relocated to Kazakhstan as a result of World War II.

Chronology

1950s	The Soviets implement the Virgin Lands program to boost agricultural production on the steppes.
1961	Yuri Gagarin, the first man in space, blasts off from the Baykonur Cosmodrome in central Kazakhstan.
1986	In Almaty and other cities, Kazakh citizens protest Moscow's appointment of an ethnic Russian to the head of the Kazakh government; an unknown number of protestors are killed.
1989	Nursultan Nazarbayev is appointed to lead the Kazakh government.
1991	Kazakhstan declares independence in December.
1993	Kazakhstan's first constitution is adopted.
1994	Legislative elections are held.
1995	The 1994 election results are declared invalid; Nazarbayev dissolves the legislature and consolidates his power by revising the constitution.
1997	The capital is moved from Almaty to Astana.
1999	President Nazarbayev is reelected in a hastily scheduled election.
2000	Kazakhstan becomes the first former Soviet republic to repay international loans.
2001	Kazakhstan joins the U.S.-led war on terrorism.
2002	Russia and Kazakhstan agree to work together on developing the oilfields beneath the Caspian Sea.
2003	Daniyal Akhmetov is named prime minister of Kazakhstan; Nazarbayev signs a law that allows for the private ownership of land.
2004	Nazarbayev approves modest reforms to the electoral process; the Otan party receives the largest number of votes in September parliamentary elections.

Glossary

antiquated—advanced in age.

autonomy—the right of self-government.

cartel—an organization of nations or businesses that controls the production and distribution of a product.

cartographer—a person who makes charts or maps.

Cold War—a period between the end of World War II and 1989, marked by intense military, economic, and political competition between the United States and the Soviet Union.

communism—a theory in which all goods and property are owned in common and are available to all as needed.

hajj—means "voyage to a sacred place" in Arabic; a religious pilgrimage that Muslims take to Mecca.

jihad—an Islamic concept of struggle against temptation and ignorance, used by extremists as justification for holy war.

Majilis—the lower chamber of Kazakhstan's legislature; its members are elected to five-year terms.

mosque—an Islamic place of worship.

mullah—an Islamic religious scholar.

oblast—an administrative province of Kazkhstan.

privatize—to turn government-owned businesses into privately owned businesses.

Qur'an—the holy book of Islam.

secular—non-religious; relating to a government that is not influenced by religious beliefs.

steppe—a vast, treeless plain.

Sufism—a sect of Islam that stresses a simple life of prayer and tolerance to achieve closeness with God.

theocracy—a state that is governed by religious principles, as interpreted by religious leaders.

zhuz—the Kazakh word for "horde" or "clan."

Further Reading

Furgus, Michael, ed. *Kazakhstan: Coming of Age.* London: Stacey International, 2004.

George, Alexandra. *Journey into Kazakhstan: The True Face of the Nazarbayev Regime.* Lanham, Md.: University Press of America, 2001.

Kleveman, Lutz. *The New Great Game: Blood and Oil in Central Asia.* New York: Atlantic Monthly Press, 2003.

Mayhew, Bradley, et al. *Lonely Planet: Central Asia,* 2nd edition. Melbourne, Australia: Lonely Planet Publications, 2000.

Nazpary, Joma. *Post-Soviet Chaos: Violence and Dispossession in Kazakhstan.* London: Pluto Press, 2001.

Olcott, Martha Brill. *Kazakhstan: Unfulfilled Promise.* Washington, D.C.: Carnegie Endowment for International Peace, 2002.

Rashid, Ahmed. *Jihad: The Rise of Militant Islam in Central Asia.* New York: Penguin Books, 2003.

Svanberg, Ingvar, ed. *Contemporary Kazaks: Cultural and Social Perspectives.* New York: St. Martin's Press, 1999.

http://www.president.kz/

The official site of Kazakhstan's president, it offers information on the country's government, economy, and history.

http://www.inform.kz/index.php?lang=eng

Maintained by Kazakhstan's national information agency, this site provides official news about all aspects of life in the country.

http://www.transparencykazakhstan.org/english/index.htm

Website of the Kazakh chapter of Transparency International, containing studies of corruption in Kazakhstan.

http://www.kazakhembus.com/

The site of Kazakhstan's embassy to the United States and Canada, with an overview of Kazakh culture and society.

http://www.osce.org/almaty/

The Almaty office of the Organization for Security and Cooperation in Europe (OSCE), which monitors political, legal, and economic developments in Kazakhstan.

http://hrw.org/doc/?t=europe&c=kazakh

News about human rights issues in Kazakhstan, provided by the group Human Rights Watch (HRW).

http://www.kazakhstanembassy.org.uk/cgi-bin/index

Maintained by the Kazakh embassy to the United Kingdom, this site provides detailed information on Kazakhstan's progress since independence.

Index

Numbers in **bold italic** refer to captions.

Index

Picture Credits

The **FOREIGN POLICY RESEARCH INSTITUTE (FPRI)** served as editorial consultants for the GROWTH AND INFLUENCE OF ISLAM IN THE NATIONS OF ASIA AND CENTRAL ASIA series. FPRI is one of the nation's oldest "think tanks." The Institute's Middle East Program focuses on Gulf security, monitors the Arab-Israeli peace process, and sponsors an annual conference for teachers on the Middle East, plus periodic briefings on key developments in the region.

Among the FPRI's trustees is a former Secretary of State and a former Secretary of the Navy (and among the FPRI's former trustees and interns, two current Undersecretaries of Defense), not to mention two university presidents emeritus, a foundation president, and several active or retired corporate CEOs.

The scholars of FPRI include a former aide to three U.S. Secretaries of State, a Pulitzer Prize–winning historian, a former president of Swarthmore College and a Bancroft Prize–winning historian, and two former staff members of the National Security Council. And the FPRI counts among its extended network of scholars—especially its Inter-University Study Groups—representatives of diverse disciplines, including political science, history, economics, law, management, religion, sociology, and psychology.

DR. HARVEY SICHERMAN is president and director of the Foreign Policy Research Institute in Philadelphia, Pennsylvania. He has extensive experience in writing, research, and analysis of U.S. foreign and national security policy, both in government and out. He served as Special Assistant to Secretary of State Alexander M. Haig Jr. and as a member of the Policy Planning Staff of Secretary of State James A. Baker III. Dr. Sicherman was also a consultant to Secretary of the Navy John F. Lehman Jr. (1982–1987) and Secretary of State George Shultz (1988).

A graduate of the University of Scranton (B.S., History, 1966), Dr. Sicherman earned his Ph.D. at the University of Pennsylvania (Political Science, 1971), where he received a Salvatori Fellowship. He is author or editor of numerous books and articles, including *America the Vulnerable: Our Military Problems and How to Fix Them* (FPRI, 2002) and *Palestinian Autonomy, Self-Government and Peace* (Westview Press, 1993). He edits *Peacefacts,* an FPRI bulletin that monitors the Arab-Israeli peace process.

JIM CORRIGAN has authored numerous newspaper and magazine articles, as well as several nonfiction books for students. A full-time freelance writer, Corrigan specializes in topics relating to history, travel, and ethnic studies. His books for young readers include *The Civil War in the West, Europeans and Native Americans,* and *Filipino Immigration.* He is a graduate of Penn State University and currently resides near Harrisburg, Pennsylvania.